Caleb Compton is an author and biosciences graduate from Redruth, Cornwall. Specialising in animal biology in his final year, he completed his degree in 2016 from the University of Exeter. His passion for animals and conservation started whilst watching nature documentaries with his family, presented by the great Sir David Attenborough. In 2013, he created a Twitter account, which brings obscure and bizarre creatures into the spotlight. Starting with just a handful of followers, it has now grown into one of the most popular animal accounts on Twitter.

For Zenan and Ferris

Caleb Compton

A BOOK OF RATHER STRANGE ANIMALS

Highlighting the Wonders of Evolution and the
Extraordinary Diversity of Life

AUSTIN MACAULEY PUBLISHERS™
LONDON • CAMBRIDGE • NEW YORK • SHARJAH

A CIP catalogue record for this title is available from the British Library.

ISBN 9781788785327 (Paperback)
ISBN 9781788785334 (Hardback)
ISBN 9781788785341 (E-Book)

www.austinmacauley.com

First Published (2019)
Austin Macauley Publishers Ltd
25 Canada Square
Canary Wharf
London
E14 5LQ

Table of Contents

Introduction

A Book of Rather Strange Animals is based on the hugely popular twitter account: @StrangeAnimals, which posts photos of fascinating, lesser-known species. This account aims to highlight the wonders of evolution and the extraordinary diversity of life. It also details the threats different species face, and the need for their conservation. This book features one hundred of the most bizarre creatures from @StrangeAnimals, providing fascinating descriptions of their behaviours and characteristics which are impossible to fit into 140 characters. The Earth is inhabited by some remarkable creatures, and this book will give you a glimpse of what this wonderful planet has to offer.

Animals are truly extraordinary. Millions of different species exist today, inhabiting every corner of the Earth. They have taken up a huge variety of forms and functions, and have masterfully adapted to their surroundings over millions of years of evolution. The first animals were marine creatures that emerged over five hundred million years ago during an event known as the 'Cambrian explosion', resulting in the rapid evolution and diversification of organisms. In the time that followed, some animals began to leave the sea and colonise the land, exploiting a vast, untouched space. The first animals to emerge from the oceans were the insects. Amphibians (which descended from fish) then took to the land and found an abundance of food in the form of land insects. Reptiles diverged from amphibians around three hundred million years ago, and their suitability to dry environments helped them spread across the land. The reptiles then gave rise to both mammals and birds, the former arising

200 million years ago and the latter 50 million years after. With the demise of the dinosaurs, countless niches were opened up, which led the way for mammals to rapidly diversify. Humans have only been around for about two hundred thousand years.

Today, animals represent an extremely diverse group of organisms. They stride on land, soar through the skies, leap from tree to tree, burrow underground, and traverse the oceans. Evolution has found a way to fill almost every conceivable niche with some kind of animal; but tragically, the survival of many species is under threat. One species of animal has decimated the Earth's natural resources and caused the destruction of many forms of life. That species is us. Our rapid population growth and dependence on non-renewable resources has led to climate change, habitat destruction, pollution, and over-hunting. These combined factors have resulted in an extinction rate that is between one thousand and ten thousand times higher than the rate of species loss before humans existed. We lose at least ten thousand species every year, although this figure is likely to be higher. In just fifty years, up to a half of all species may become extinct. Conservation is a hugely important issue, but many people are unaware of it. However, we do have an opportunity to prevent the destruction of our planet's biodiversity by changing our attitudes and policies towards nature. The time to act is now.

Everyone knows about the plight of the tiger, or the giant panda, but who knows about the endangered purple frog, or golden snub-nosed monkey? Who is aware that the saiga antelope is on the verge of extinction? This book hopes to bring light upon the perils faced by unfamiliar and obscure creatures, so that we can protect them for future generations. There is beauty and wonder in every species, and this book will show you why.

Strange Animals

Star-Nosed Mole:

The star-nosed mole *(Condylura cristata)* lives in eastern and northern America and has twenty-two highly sensitive tentacles located on its nose. The mole uses these fleshy projections to find prey underground. The tentacles can detect electrical impulses emitted by prey, and are also extremely receptive to touch. This unique organ also blocks soil and food from entering the mole's nostrils. These tentacles have over twenty-five thousand sensory organs per square centimetre (called Eimer's organs) which might be able to sense seismic waves.

The star-nosed mole measures twenty centimetres from snout to tail and eats worms, leeches, frogs and insects. It can find and eat food in just 0.12 seconds, which makes it the quickest eater out of any mammal. They are good swimmers, and have the ability to smell underwater by creating air bubbles before sucking them up through their nostrils. This allows them to pick up scents whilst diving. During the breeding season, the males' testicles can weigh roughly ten percent of their overall bodyweight. These moles are preyed upon by a wide variety of animals such as birds of prey, skunks, weasels and large fish, but are under no threat from humans.

Leafy Seadragon:

The leafy seadragon (*Phycodurus eques*) can be found on the southern and eastern coasts of Australia, in waters up to fifty metres deep. These magnificent creatures have some of the most elaborate camouflages in the animal kingdom. They measure up to twenty-four centimetres long, and have a collection of yellow or brown leaf-like appendages covering their bodies. These appendages hide them well amongst the kelp, seaweed and seagrass that grows in shallow coastal waters. The fish has tiny, transparent fins which beat very slightly to avoid attracting attention from predators. Because of the size of its fins, the fish moves extremely slowly through the water, appearing to drift in the current like seaweed. It is also able to change its colour based on its surroundings.

Leafy seadragons eat small shrimp, amphipods and plankton which are sucked up through their pipe-shaped mouth. Like their close relative the seahorse, males look after the eggs, which are placed onto his tail by the female, and then attach to the male's brood patch, remaining there until they hatch nine weeks later. This is a threatened species, which is often caught for the aquarium trade, and for use in alternative 'medicine'. Pollution and habitat loss also pose a big risk to the future of the species.

Giraffe Weevil:

Giraffe weevils (*Trachelophorus giraffa*) are native to Madagascar and measure 2.5 centimetres. This species has a bright red wing case and a black body, but the most prominent feature is its absurdly long neck, that is used for fighting and building intricate nests. Males have a much larger neck, which can be up to three times as long as the female's! When two males are fighting, the female will wait nearby for the champion to emerge and will even act as a sort of 'referee' during the fight.

After the fighting has ended, and mating has occurred, the female carefully cuts a leaf and folds up the end where she lays a single egg. The leaf is then chewed off and drops to the forest floor where it will eventually hatch, and the larvae inside get their nutrients from their plant cocoon. The weevil is very picky when it comes to nesting material, and only uses leaves from two closely related tree species. They also feed exclusively on these trees, and spend most of their lives on their branches.

Common Gliding Lizard:

The common gliding lizard (*Draco sumatranus*) from Southeast Asia is a real-life dragon! Well, kind of. This lizard has elongated ribs that extend into a wing membrane, allowing it to glide for great distances. Gliding is a big advantage for these animals, as it helps them get away from predators very quickly. There are forty-two species of gliding lizards, which spend most of their lives in the trees.

Only females leave the relative safety of the canopy, so they can lay their eggs in the ground. The common gliding lizard feeds mainly on ants and termites and reaches just nine centimetres in length. Males have a yellow 'throat flag' called a gular fold, which is used for communication, and to attract mates. Females also have a fold, but it's much smaller and blue in colour. Although these lizards can't actually fly, they can travel an impressive sixty metres through the air during a single glide! Their gliding membrane and ribs can be extended like a fan, and it's folded close to the body when not in use. Some species of gliding lizard can change their colour slightly to match the patterns and colours of different tree trunks. The lizard's population trends are currently not known, although deforestation may be affecting their numbers.

Marvellous Spatuletail:

The marvellous spatuletail (*Loddigesia mirabilis*) is a rare hummingbird native to the Río Utcubamba region of Peru.

Only males of the species have these long, beautiful tails, which are used to attract the opposite sex. A mature male grows to fifteen centimetres and his tail can be up to four times the size of his body! The tail is made up of just four feathers, a feature not found in any other bird. When a female is spotted, males rapidly wave their two blue discs or 'spatules' whilst hovering in front of her. The aim of this display is to show that they are strong, and are suitable partners for mating. It costs a huge amount of energy to perform this mating dance, and for this reason, males can't sustain the display for long.

Unfortunately, the bird's tail also stands out to local people who hunt them with slingshots, which means a lot more males are killed than females. This (along with deforestation for the illegal drug trade) has resulted in a great decline in numbers of the marvellous spatuletail, and it is now classified as an endangered species. A large-scale conservation operation was launched in 2006 to protect the hummingbird's habitat by planting thousands of native trees in the region.

Water Opossum:

Found in the streams and lakes of Latin America is the water opossum, or yapok (*Chironectes minimus*), which is the only aquatic marsupial on Earth. It has several adaptations to an aquatic lifestyle, such as water-resistant fur, a long tail for swimming, and even webbed feet! Its front paws aren't webbed, but are used to sense and catch prey. Bristles and whiskers on its face help detect predators and aid in navigation.

The water opossum grows to around thirty centimetres in length, and sleeps in small burrows in stream banks during the day. At night, it hunts for crabs, fish, crustaceans and other small animals it can find in the water. Females have a pouch where they keep their babies, and strong pouch muscles allow the mother to keep her young dry, even whilst diving underwater. Males also possess a pouch, which is used to store their genitals before entering the water, so that they are more streamlined when swimming. The male's pouch also reduces the risk of getting their penis caught in aquatic plants. Water opossums are the only marsupial alive today where males have a pouch. According to the International Union for Conservation of Nature (IUCN), the opossum's numbers are falling, although it is regarded as 'Least Concern', meaning that they are not presently at risk of extinction. However, mining operations may endanger local populations by impacting water quality, and they are also hunted in some areas.

Beluga Whale:

Belugas (*Delphinapterus leucas*) are white-skinned whales found in the Arctic and sub-Arctic oceans. They grow to over five metres long, weigh up to 1600 kilograms, and possess a gigantic, bulbous head that houses an echolocation organ called 'the melon'. This organ can produce a beam of sound waves that help the whale navigate around ice, find air pockets and hunt prey. The beluga's diet consists mainly of fish, crabs and molluscs, and they can dive seven hundred metres to find food. They uncover burrowing prey by spitting a stream of water at the seafloor, forcing away the silt surrounding them. Their unusual white colour acts as a camouflage, allowing the whales to blend into the surrounding polar ice caps. Despite measuring over five metres, belugas are some of the smallest whales and are hunted by apex predators such as orcas and polar bears.

Another unique feature of the beluga is that it seasonally sheds its skin and will rub itself on gravel riverbeds in order to remove it. The whale's blubber makes up about forty percent of its bodyweight, which protects it from the freezing waters it inhabits. Belugas are one of the most sociable whales, and often travel and hunt in pods of hundreds of individuals. They carry objects on their backs during the breeding season such as wood, nets and bones, and they play with bubbles or random objects in the water. The beluga's main threats include hunting, disease and pollution.

Armoured Searobin:

The armoured searobin (*Peristediidae*) or armoured gurnard is a strange deep-sea fish that lives in tropical waters around the world, at depths between 150 and 900 metres. There are forty-five species of armoured searobin, which are adorned with thick scales and spikes for protection against predators. This bizarre fish can detect prey using sensory organs called barbels, which are located under its chin. It can also dig around in the sea floor using its elongated nose, searching for burrowing animals.

The armoured searobin feeds on shrimp, crustaceans and small fish. They are crimson-red in colour, and can measure up to thirty-five centimetres from head to tail. They appear to crawl along the sea floor using four specialised 'fin spines' on the underside of their bodies, which look like crab legs. These spines are not actually used for walking, but instead, help detect prey. Chemoreceptors present in the spines locate amino acids in the water, which are produced by the fish's prey, allowing the creature to home in on its target.

Purple Frog:

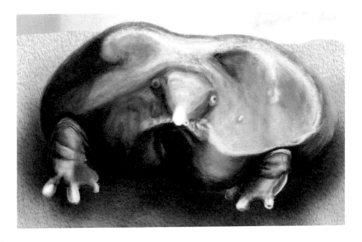

The Western Ghats of India is one of the most biologically diverse areas on Earth, and is home to the unusual purple frog (*Nasikabatrachus sahyadrensis*). Purple frogs have been geographically isolated for millions of years, and are the sole surviving members from a family of amphibians that flourished over 130 million years ago. They spend most of their time in burrows underground (which can be up to four metres deep), only emerging to mate for several weeks every year, during the monsoon. Males use a sticky substance to glue themselves to the female before mating. Due to their subterranean lifestyle, the adult frogs weren't formally documented until 2003 (but the tadpoles were discovered way back in 1918).

The purple frog feeds on termites, sucking them up with a hoover-like tongue. It has a round body, small face and a pointy nose. It measures seven centimetres in length, and has a loud call which apparently sounds like the clucking of a chicken. Tadpoles have powerful mouth suckers which allow them to stick onto the riverbed during strong currents. The purple frog is an extremely rare species, and is classed as endangered. It's threatened by habitat loss and the proposed construction of several dams, which could flood their natural habitat. A closely related species was discovered in August 2017 and was named Bhupathy's purple frog (*Nasikabatrachus bhupathi*).

Large Flying Fox:

The large flying fox (*Pteropus vampyrus*) is an enormous megabat that is endemic to Southeast Asia. It measures up to thirty-two centimetres in length, weighs over a kilogram, and has a wingspan of 1.5 metres, making it one of the largest bats in the world. It is named for its fox-like appearance, and nests in trees in enormous groups of over ten thousand individuals! These giant bats feed on fruit and nectar and will fly up to fifty kilometres from their nesting areas in the search for food. Foraging occurs at night, and they rest during the day. When it is particularly hot, they will lick themselves to cool down and use their wings as a fan. There are sixty species of flying fox, and they are all important jungle pollinators, helping to disperse the seeds of many tropical plants across Asia. Sadly, these bats have suffered a considerable decline in recent years due to forest degradation, and overhunting for food and sport. More than half of all flying fox species now face extinction.

Stalk-Eyed Fly:

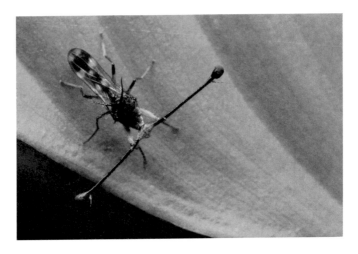

There are around 160 species of stalk-eyed fly (*Diopsidae*) which can be found on every continent apart from Antarctica. They measure up to one centimetre in length, and feed on the bacteria and fungi that grow on rotting animals and plants. These insects have bizarre eyes that are mounted on the end of long stalks, extending outwards from the sides of the head. In some species, the eyestalks can actually be longer than the fly's entire body! Eyestalks are an advantage when it comes to vision, but they pose a problem during flight, as they reduce aerodynamics and increase the fly's weight. This characteristic probably evolved because females prefer males with longer stalks, as it signifies good health.

Males compete for territory, and those with bigger stalks scare off smaller rivals. If two males with eyestalks of equal length meet, they will fight by punching each other with their front legs. After the stalk-eyed fly hatches from its pupa case, it will suck air into its mouth, and then push it through tubes in its head, causing the stalks to extend outwards. They must do this right after they hatch, as their tissues are still soft and inflatable.

Malayan Tapir:

The Malayan tapir (*Tapirus indicus)* is a large, pig-like mammal that lives in the forests of Southeast Asia. It is the biggest species of tapir, with a body length of 2.5 metres and a bodyweight of up to 540 kilograms! It has a very long and flexible nose (similar to an elephant's) which it uses to reach tall plants. They are herbivores and have been observed eating 122 different plant species. Compared to their body, they have one of the largest penises of any animal, which is oddly shaped to grip females whilst mating. Their penis is so unique that there are even scientific papers written about it!

Tapirs are born after a year in the womb, and have mottled fur which acts as camouflage, mimicking light passing through the leaves to the forest floor. When threatened, tapirs will run at high speeds and often bite aggressors with their powerful jaws. In 1998, a zoo employee had his whole arm ripped off by a tapir who was defending her baby at the Oklahoma City Zoo. There are five species of tapir, and out of the four that have been evaluated, all are either endangered or vulnerable to extinction. Malayan tapirs have become endangered from large-scale deforestation and hunting by humans.

Sea Pig:

The sea pig (*Scotoplanes*) is a deep-sea echinoderm that lives at tremendous depths of up to six thousand metres! This peculiar animal is actually a type of sea cucumber, and is named after its fat, pink body which looks like a pig. They grow to about fifteen centimetres and walk along the seafloor using special appendages called 'tube feet'. The sea pig can have up to seven pairs of tube feet, and move by inflating and deflating them. They also have sensory tentacles on the top of their bodies which help them find food. This strange creature eats any organic material that settles in the mud on the seafloor. This could be small scraps of leftover food that shallower-dwelling animals didn't manage to eat, or even whole whale carcasses. They often gather in groups of over a hundred to devour a large meal.

Sea pigs have the ability to breathe through their skin, and they also host several gruesome parasites, such as crustaceans and sea snails, which bore into their bodies and feed on the sea pig's insides! Four species of sea pig have been discovered, and they are one of the most abundant organisms in the deep-sea. Trawling is the main threat to this species, and a decrease in the sea pig population can potentially be very harmful for other deep-sea animals, especially their predators.

Philippine Flying Lemur:

Philippine flying lemurs, or colugos, (*Cynocephalus volans*) are tree-dwelling mammals from the southern islands of the Philippines. They measure up to forty centimetres in length and their tail is almost as long as their body. They are not actually lemurs (or even primates) and they can't fly; however, they are able to glide exceptionally well. They have a large, kite-shaped membrane that allows them to travel over one hundred metres through the air! This gliding membrane also acts as a sort of pouch for their babies, which develop there over six months in a similar way to marsupials. Flying lemurs can use their membrane as a cloak, as its colouring is very similar to bark. During the day, the animal clings to branches, or hides in the holes of tree trunks. At night, they forage for flowers and leaves. These creatures are hunted by large birds such as eagles, which easily catch them when they are slowly gliding through the forest. It is thought that up to ninety percent of the Philippine eagle's diet is flying lemurs! There are two species of flying lemur, and they are very close relatives of primates. Both species have suffered a decline in numbers because of habitat destruction and hunting.'

Trilobite Beetle:

Trilobite beetles (*Platerodrilus*) are a fascinating group of insects found in the forests of India and Southeast Asia. Females of this species have armour casing and a tiny head, which can be retracted into the body for protection. They have huge scales covering their bodies that resemble the prehistoric arthropods of the same name. These beetles come in a variety of colours such as orange, black, purple, pink or brown. Males look completely different to females, and measure just eight millimetres long. Females are on average ten times bigger than the males and look the same as larvae, because they do not develop a cocoon or undergo metamorphosis. This means that they keep their larval form as an adult. In contrast, males transform from the larval stage and look like ordinary, small beetles as adults (with large wing cases and antennae). In fact, the males are so different that they look like a completely separate species! Over twenty types of trilobite beetle have been discovered so far.

Hummingbird Bobtail Squid:

Humming-bird bobtail squid (*Euprymna berryi*) inhabit the coastal waters of the Indo-Pacific. Females are just five centimetres long and the males are even smaller. Their bodies contain millions of light-reflecting cells called chromatophores, which decorate the squid with marvellous shades of bright blue, green and purple. They feed on small crustaceans at night, and hide in soft sediment on the seafloor during the day. The squid has an extraordinary adaptation to avoid predation, using bioluminescent bacteria inside its body to hide its silhouette. Inside its body wall, there is a specialised light organ that contains bacteria which emit just the right amount of light to remove the squid's shadow from the view of potential predators. The intensity of light given off by the bacteria is the same as the light that hits the top of the squid's body. The squid even uses filters to control the amount of light emitted by the bacteria, so it can adjust for moonlight or sunlight. The light-emitting bacteria also benefit from living inside the squid as they feed on a sugar solution it produces. Every morning, the humming-bird bobtail squid expels ninety-five percent of its bacteria, and slowly regains them during the day. Scientists are not quite sure why they do this, although it may be because it is energetically costly to store them during the day.

Lygodium Spider Moth:

Another master of disguise is the Lygodium spider moth (*Siamusotima aranea*) from Thailand. This species (which was only discovered in 2005) has evolved to mimic one of the scariest creatures in the animal kingdom: the arachnid. On each of its white wings is a set of four brown bands that look like the legs of a crab spider! When threatened, the moth stretches out its wings to display its spidery markings, frightening off potential predators. If that wasn't enough to deter attackers, it also has protective armour near its back: a feature not present on any other moth that we know of. The larvae of this species are quite unique too, as they resemble beetle larvae and have an 'anal shield' which protects them from parasites and predators. This creature is named after the Lygodium climbing fern which it spends most of its time feeding on. This plant has become a huge pest in Florida, taking over wetlands and altering the environment dramatically. It is thought that the Lygodium spider moth could be used as a biological control there, halting the spread of this invasive fern.

Mata Mata Turtle:

Found in the freshwater lakes and rivers of South America is the mata mata turtle (*Chelus fimbriatus*), which has a shell length of forty-five centimetres and weighs around fifteen kilograms. Large flaps of skin are present on the neck and head, and it has an elongated, snorkel-like nose. The turtle's rough shell looks like bark, and its oddly shaped head resembles a collection of dead leaves. This provides efficient camouflage in its aquatic home.

The mata mata is an ambush predator that lurks in rivers and lakes waiting for unlucky fish to swim past. It has a strange feeding technique called suction feeding, where it produces a 'low-pressure vacuum' with its huge mouth. The turtle hides in the murky waters, completely motionless until a fish approaches. Then it lurches its head forward with its mouth wide open and its throat extended. A small vacuum is created and the fish gets sucked into the turtle's mouth. The mata mata then spits out the water, and gulps down the fish without even chewing it! Skin flaps on its head may be used to sense the vibrations of potential prey. Due to its widespread distribution and lack of threats, this species is not currently considered to be endangered.

Pink Fairy Armadillo:

The pink fairy armadillo, or pichiciego (*Chlamyphorus truncatus*) is the smallest of the twenty-one armadillo species alive today. They grow to just eleven centimetres and weigh 120 grams. Pink armoured shells protect them from attackers, and their soft white hair aids in thermoregulation. Like other armadillos, they curl into a ball when threatened. This species is found only in the deserts of central Argentina, and spends almost its entire life underground, hunting for burrowing insects and munching on vegetation. The only time it emerges from the ground is during a storm, as it might drown if it remains belowground. It has huge front claws in relation to its body, which it uses to shift dirt quickly. As with other burrowing animals, it has poor eyesight, but it makes up for that with its heightened sense of touch and hearing. Their flat bottoms compact dirt behind them whilst burrowing, which stops their tunnels collapsing. Internal body temperature is controlled by pumping blood around the soft shell (which also gives it its pink colour).

The pink fairy armadillo is a rare animal that is hardly ever seen, and relatively unstudied. Although its conservation status is uncertain, we do know that it has declined recently due to farming and predation by dogs and cats.

Acorn Weevil:

The acorn weevil (*Curculio nucum*) is a small beetle from Europe, measuring eight millimetres in length. It has an unusual, elongated snout or 'rostrum' which is actually longer than its body! At the end of this massive snout are a small pair of jaws. These are used to drill into acorns to extract the nice fatty liquids inside, which are sucked up through the rostrum. The weevil also lays its egg inside the acorn, and makes sure that there are enough nutrients left for its young when it hatches. After depositing a single egg into the nut, the weevil seals up the hole with its own faeces! The acorn not only provides a food source for the larva, but it also protects it from predators during the most vulnerable stage of its life. When the nut falls from the tree, the weevil larva inside starts to eat its way out. When the larva finally emerges, it buries itself underground and develops into a pupa. It will remain underground for several years, until it grows into a fully-sized adult. There are thirty species of nut weevil, which infest different types of nut and are considered a pest in some areas.

Christmas Frigatebird:

The Christmas frigatebird (*Fregata andrewsi*) is a critically endangered seabird found only on Christmas Island: a small territory in the Indian Ocean. It has a wingspan of over two metres, and only weighs about a kilogram, which means that flying requires very little energy. For this reason, it is capable of sustaining flight for up to a week without landing!

Males pump air into a skin pouch found on their necks, which creates a weird throat balloon known as a 'gular sac'. This huge, bright-red sac takes about twenty minutes to fully inflate, and is used for attracting females during the breeding season.

These birds have a curious feeding technique, where they harass other birds so that they throw up, and then eat the victim's regurgitated food (a process called kleptoparasitism). As well as eating vomit, the Christmas frigatebird also hunts fish and squid from the surface of the ocean. Their most common prey is flying fish, which are snapped up as they burst out of the water to glide. They are also cannibals, feeding on other frigatebirds' eggs and chicks! Surprisingly, the main threat to the survival of this species is an invasive insect called the yellow crazy ant (*Anoplolepis gracilipes*). These ants destroy the birds' native trees and reduce available nesting sites. This is a huge problem because the bird has only three breeding populations and requires very specific nesting conditions.

Fiji Crested Iguana:

The Fiji crested iguana (*Brachylophus vitiensis*) is a critically endangered lizard, endemic to the dry forests of the

Fijian islands. They are one of the most geographically isolated iguanas in the world, arriving on the islands long ago, after floating on vegetation over nine thousand kilometres across the Pacific Ocean. Their closest relatives live in the Americas. The Fiji crested iguana reaches seventy-five centimetres in length, and has large spikes running down its spine. They are vegetarians and feed on fruit, leaves and flowers. Their bodies are a vivid green, and males are covered in white bands (females are solid green). Hatchlings are dark in colour, but transform to light green after only a few hours. Eggs hatch after nine months, which is the longest incubation time of any iguana.

When threatened, the Fiji crested iguana will undergo a colour change from green to black. This process is very quick, and usually scares off predators. If this doesn't work, they will make themselves look bigger and often launch themselves at the attacker. This animal is under threat from habitat loss and the presence of invasive species on their island home. Feral cats hunt the iguanas, invasive goats compete with them for food, and introduced Leucaena trees reduce the iguanas' natural food source. This has resulted in a major ecological disturbance, and has brought the iguana to the edge of extinction.

Longlure Frogfish:

36

The longlure frogfish (*Antennarius multiocellatus*) from the western Atlantic Ocean is the fastest animal on the planet. Antennariidae (the group of fish known as frogfish) have been recorded catching and swallowing prey in as little as six milliseconds! They hide in reefs, and blend in perfectly to their environment, changing colour to match the different types of coral nearby. Markings on their bodies mimic the holes of sponges.

The longlure uses a specialised fin spine as a fishing rod, attracting prey into striking distance. It waits at the bottom of the seafloor, shaking its rod to mimic the movements of a small crustacean or fish. When its prey approaches, the frogfish thrusts out its head and engulfs its victim at lightning speed, which is the fastest recorded movement of any animal. They hunt fish, shrimp, crabs and even other frogfish! The longlure frogfish can expand its mouth up to twelve times, and it can also expand its stomach, allowing it to swallow fish much larger than itself! They measure up to twenty centimetres in length, and live in the warm waters of the western Atlantic. Their general movement is very slow, and they walk along the seafloor using modified fins.

Goblin Shark:

Goblin sharks (*Mitsukurina owstoni*) are extraordinary creatures that inhabit the deep sea, over one thousand metres from the surface. They have elongated noses and pink, rubbery skin, and can grow to over six metres in length! Due to their primitive-looking features, they are referred to as 'living fossils', and are rarely seen by humans. Millions of sensors are located on the shark's nose which can detect electric currents produced by other organisms in the water. Its mouth contains an extendable jaw, which can be released quickly using elastic ligaments. It hunts in the deep, dark waters for crustaceans, fish and squid. When searching for prey, the goblin shark drifts slowly with minimum effort, avoiding detection. When it gets close enough to its target, it shoots out its jaw, and either catches it in its mouth, or sucks it in. Scientists believe this strange jaw mechanism evolved because they are slow swimmers and struggle to pursue faster prey. Inside the goblin shark's extendable mouth lies up to sixty-two rows of nail-like teeth, which curve backwards to stop its prey from escaping. Despite their formidable appearance, they pose no threat to humans. The shark resides in mostly unfished waters, although some are accidently caught by trawlers and gillnets.

Shoebill:

The shoebill or whalehead (*Balaeniceps rex*) is a large wading bird from the marshes and swamps of tropical Africa. These prehistoric-looking creatures have grey or blue plumage and possess a powerful beak that is twenty centimetres long and ten centimetres wide. They stand at 1.5 metres tall and have a wingspan of 2.6 metres! An ambush predator, the shoebill will stand completely still in the water waiting for fish, and strikes at prey extremely fast. As well as fish, they will hunt water snakes, turtles and even small crocodiles! Their immense beak both crushes and shatters prey in an instant, and they can even decapitate their prey in one swift move.

After mating, both sexes help to construct a nest, and will guard it aggressively from other shoebills. Males will stay with the female after the eggs are laid, and will help protect and incubate them. They also assist in feeding the hatchlings, regurgitating food directly into their mouths. Females lay two or three eggs, but only one will survive to adulthood because of a lack of food. The second or third chicks are usually kept as a 'backup' in case the firstborn dies, or is too weak. The parents will focus their attention on the biggest chick, and will often starve the others. The larger chick is also very aggressive to its siblings. Shoebills have lost much of their historic habitat and are classed as a vulnerable species. They are threatened by hunting, habitat loss and pollution.

Tongue-Eating Louse:

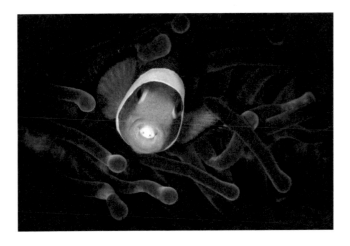

The tongue-eating louse (*Cymothoa exigua*) is a nightmare-inducing isopod that devours the tongue of a fish and then replaces it with its own body! It is the only known parasite to completely replace a host's organ. This gruesome process starts when immature lice get inside the gills of an unsuspecting rose snapper, which is where they develop into males. After some time, one louse changes sex to become a female, and makes its way into the snapper's mouth. It then bites the fish's tongue, and sucks all the blood out of it, causing the organ to atrophy and fall off. After getting rid of the tongue, the parasite latches onto the stump with its four pairs of strong legs. From here on, the louse acts as the snapper's tongue, grinding up food for its host. The louse eats bits of food that the snapper ingests, and also feeds on the fish's blood and mucus. The other males left inside the gills will come out of their hiding place every now and then to mate with the female, inside the snapper's mouth! A brood of immature male lice are born and then spat out by the host fish, ready to carry on this disgusting lifecycle. There are many species of *Cymothoa* and they parasitize a wide variety of fish. They are found throughout the world's oceans, and adults measure three centimetres long.

Flannel Moth Caterpillar:

The flannel moth caterpillar (*Megalopyge opercularis*) is native to the southeast United States, Mexico and Central America. This fluffy-looking creature appears to have soft fur, but you wouldn't want to pet it as it has an extremely painful sting, and is one of the most toxic caterpillars in North America. It has thousands of poisonous barbs hidden under its hairs that can result in agonizing pain that can last for up to twelve hours. The barbs lodge themselves in the skin, and if they are not removed, they can continue to release venom over the course of several hours. A sting from this insect may even lead to vomiting, difficulty breathing and chest pain. People who have been unlucky enough to get stung have described the pain as being worse than a broken bone. That's quite impressive for a caterpillar that measures less than three centimetres long!

The sting of the flannel moth caterpillar is so bad that a bird called the cinereous mourner (*Laniocera hypopyrra*) mimics the insect as a baby to avoid being attacked by predators! These chicks have fluffy yellow hairs, and even bob their heads slowly to imitate the caterpillar's movements.

This unusual camouflage is the only known case of a mammal mimicking an insect.

Turtle Frog:

The turtle frog (*Myobatrachus gouldii*) is a small, stocky amphibian from Western Australia which looks a bit like a turtle without a shell. They measure about five centimetres in length and have strong, muscular front legs which help them dig through the earth, and break termite mounds. They have small eyes and short limbs, and their heads are tiny compared to the rest of their bodies. The diet of the turtle frog consists entirely of termites, and they will eat hundreds in one sitting.

Before mating, turtle frogs construct tunnels measuring up to a metre in length. Both males and females take part in the creation of the tunnels, where they will live together for the next four months, sheltering from the extreme heat. Later in the year, the couple will mate and the female will lay up to forty eggs underground. They wait so long to mate so that their eggs will hatch during the wet season, and their offspring won't be at risk of drying out. Turtle frogs skip the tadpole stage entirely, developing into fully formed frogs whilst inside their eggs. It is thought that they miss this stage to avoid heavy predation of the tadpoles. This unusual amphibian is the only member of the genus *Myobatrachus*, and it is not currently threatened by humans.

Penis Snake:

This bizarre creature is known as the penis snake (*Atretochoana eiselti*) or 'man-aconda' and is native to the rainforests of Brazil. Although it does have a strong resemblance to a human penis, it is not actually a snake, and isn't even related to them. In fact, the penis snake is a type of limbless amphibian called a caecilian. These creatures are found in the tropics, spending most of their time underground. Baby caecilians feed on the skin of their mother, although she is unharmed in the process.

The penis snake is a rare species that grows to at least eighty centimetres, and spends its whole life in water. It is thought to eat worms and small fish. Most caecilians have at least one well-developed lung, but the penis snake doesn't have any. Therefore, it is the biggest four-limbed animal that doesn't have lungs. Its nostrils are completely sealed, and instead of breathing through its mouth, this amphibian takes in oxygen through capillaries in its skin! Their skin is very wrinkly, which increases the overall surface area for gas exchange. This species was discovered in the late 1800s, but only two specimens were known until it was rediscovered by accident in 2011. Due to its secretive nature, not much is known about the biology of the penis snake, and its conservation status is yet to be evaluated.

Hummingbird Hawk-Moth:

The hummingbird hawk-moth (*Macroglossum stellatarum*) can be found in warm climates in southern Europe, North Africa and parts of Asia. It is fairly large for a moth, with a wingspan of about five centimetres, and it is often mistaken for a hummingbird. These insects beat their wings so quickly that they produce a humming sound, and they use their long proboscis to extract nectar from flowers.

When feeding, they hover in the air and their long hairs look like a bird's feathers.

The hummingbird hawk-moth can beat its wings at an astonishing eighty-five times per second! It has a fantastic memory, and will visit the same patch of flowers every day at the same time! Their eggs mimic the flower buds of the bedstraw plant, which keeps them safe from predators. The moth's extraordinary resemblance to the hummingbird is an example of convergent evolution: where similar characteristics evolve in different species that aren't closely related, due to them living in similar conditions.

Greater Blue-Ringed Octopus:

The greater blue-ringed octopus (*Hapalochlaena lunulata*) is a tiny, but extremely dangerous cephalopod from the Indian and Pacific oceans. It has an arm span of ten centimetres and weighs eighty grams on average. Despite its small size, it is capable of delivering one of the most potent toxins known to mammals. Normally beige in colour, its skin will produce up to sixty neon blue rings when agitated. These rings pulsate and serve as a warning to predators. For humans, a bite from the octopus will cause the muscles in the body to shut down, preventing breathing, and can result in death by respiratory arrest. The octopus' venom is a thousand times more potent than cyanide and there is enough of it in their bodies to kill twenty-six adult humans at once! There is no known antidote to the venom, but due to its shy nature, it rarely comes into contact with humans. Only three deaths have been reported by this creature. Blue-ringed octopuses have a second type of venom, which is secreted from a separate gland and is used for hunting. They camouflage themselves against the sea floor, wiggling one tentacle like a worm to lure small crabs and shrimp. They will then immobilise their victims by biting them with their sharp beaks, and injecting their secondary venom.

Honeypot Ant:

Ants are incredible organisms, forming immense colonies that can contain several million individuals. Many have adapted to specific roles which provide a crucial service to their fellow workers. One of the more bizarre roles is that of the honeypot ant. These specialised workers can be found in the colonies of many different ant species and usually inhabit hot, dry environments such as Mexico, South Africa and Australia. The ants are fattened up by other workers until their abdomens are swollen with a nutrient-rich liquid. These are known as repletes and they are basically living food storage containers. Normal workers in the colony feed on the stored liquid when resources are low. The honeypot ants hang from the ceilings of tunnels, and when another ant is hungry, it will approach the honeypot and caress its antennae, which causes it to vomit up a portion of its food supply. They get their nutrient-rich liquids by feeding on desert flowers which contain sugary nectar. This form of food storage has developed in at least thirty-four different ant species. Honeypot repletes are extremely valuable in the insect world, and some species of ants invade other colonies to steal their honeypots and make them their slaves!

Great Potoo:

The great potoo (*Nyctibius grandis*) is a strange, owl-like bird that is camouflaged to look like tree bark so that it can blend in with its forest surroundings. During the day they perch on tree stumps, appearing to be just another part of the tree. They make nests on these stumps, laying a single egg inside. Both the female and male help incubate the egg, and raise the offspring after it hatches. This species inhabits dense, lowland forests from southern Mexico to Brazil. They have a large head and huge eyes, and its unique call has been described as scary and unsettling.

Potoos are nocturnal animals, and do all their hunting at night. Their diet consists mainly of insects, but they are also quite fond of bats. Great potoos are predated upon by tayras (a type of weasel) and falcons, and their eggs are eaten by several species of monkey. If they are spotted by a predator, they will instantly change to a 'freeze' posture, which makes them look even more like a stump. The population of great potoos has dropped over the past few decades because of deforestation, and this remains a major hazard to this species.

Fangtooth Moray Eel:

The fangtooth moray eel or tiger moray (*Enchelycore anatine*) grows to 1.2 metres long and has two rows of sharp, crystal-like teeth which are slightly transparent. It has been nicknamed the tiger moray due to its bright yellow and brown colouration. It is common in the waters of the Mediterranean and East Atlantic, although it is relatively hard to find because of its elusive behaviour. This menacing-looking fish generally poses no danger to humans, but they have given a nasty bite to divers who provoke them!

Fangtooth morays live in crevices and caves on rocky seafloors, about fifty metres deep, where they wait for prey. They are active predators, and feed on shrimp, molluscs, small fish, and other small crustaceans. Despite its reputation as a fearsome carnivore, the eel is often spotted with a Pacific cleaner shrimp (*Lysmata amboinensis*) scuttling around in its mouth, which eats the eel's dead tissues and parasites. The shrimp is left to do its work on the eel's mouth and is unharmed in the process.

Bargibant's Seahorse:

Found in coastal areas of the Indian and Central Pacific oceans is one of the tiniest seahorses on the planet. It's called Bargibant's seahorse (*Hippocampus bargibanti*) and measures less than two centimetres from head to tail. These fish have a well-developed camouflage, hiding away on gorgonian corals. They grab hold of these structures using their prehensile tails, and have nodules on their bodies which mimic the coral's polyps. They spend their entire lives on this specific coral: feeding, breeding and raising their young there.

They are so well-hidden that they were only discovered when scientists were closely analysing gorgonian corals in the lab, and a couple of seahorses fell off.

Nine pygmy seahorse species have been discovered so far, and the smallest is just 1.4 centimetres tall! Bargibant's seahorse is a bit larger at two centimetres, and has two different colour morphs which match specific coral. Although their diets are not fully understood, they likely eat microscopic crustaceans and zooplankton. Little is also known about their conservation status, but they may be taken from the wild for the aquarium trade. It is hoped that new environmental laws in Australia will allow the animal to continue to thrive in its habitat.

New Caledonian Giant Gecko:

The largest gecko on Earth is the New Caledonian giant gecko (*Rhacodactylus leachianus*), growing up to thirty-six centimetres long! They have evolved this impressive size due to a process called 'island gigantism', where a lack of predators allows small organisms to grow much larger than their mainland relatives. These geckos are found on New

Caledonia: an isolated group of islands in the Pacific that are over a thousand kilometres away from the coast of Australia.

New Caledonian giant geckos are described as having short tails, chubby bodies and loose, wrinkly skin. They have a varied diet: eating fruit, nectar, insects, sap and other geckos. They are active during the night and shelter in holes and crevices during the day, and occasionally bask in the sun. When threatened, they produce a loud growling sound. Although its conservation status has been assessed as Least Concern by the IUCN, the New Caledonian giant gecko is under threat from introduced species, habitat loss, and other human activities.

Vaquita:

The vaquita, or cochito (*Phocoena sinus*), is a tiny and extremely rare porpoise that inhabits a very limited zone in the Gulf of California. It has dark patches around the eyes, and adults measure just 135 centimetres in length, making it the smallest cetacean in the world! They hunt fish, octopus and squid using echolocation. They are very shy animals, and will quickly vanish when approached by a boat.

The vaquita is also the most endangered cetacean in the world, and is classified as critically endangered. The main threat to this animal comes in the form of illegal gillnet fishing, which accidentally traps and kills vaquitas as bycatch. Despite the Mexican government's ban on this method of fishing, and the creation of a protected area in the porpoise's habitat, gillnet fishing is still occurring in the area. As of March 2018, it is estimated that the porpoise's numbers have plummeted to just a dozen individuals. It is predicted that without drastic action being taken, this beautiful creature may become extinct by the end of 2018. Indeed, by the time you read this book, the vaquita might have vanished from existence.

Shingleback Lizard:

Shinglebacks (*Tiliqua rugosa*) are medium-sized lizards native to drier regions of southern Australia. They grow to about forty centimetres, and have a heavy armour in the form of thick scales. It has a huge head compared to the rest of its body, and a stubby tail which stores fat that is used in winter and during droughts. The shingleback has a large, blue tongue and a bright-pink mouth, which is used as a defence mechanism against predators. When the lizard senses an animal, such as a snake or bird, it will turn towards the attacker and open its mouth wide. This, along with the size of the lizard's head, scares away most predators. If this first line of defence fails, they press their bodies flat on the ground and hiss loudly. The shingleback's tail resembles a head which serves to confuse predators, and can prevent the lizard from receiving a fatal head wound. They are also capable of administering a painful bite if picked up. The lizard eats insects and plant matter, such as flowers, and also scavenges off dead animals. Surprisingly, shinglebacks mate with the same partner every year for over twenty years. This long-term pairing is very rare in lizards. The offspring are massive compared to their mother, measuring half the size of the adult at birth!

Picasso Bug:

This species of shield-backed bug looks like a beautiful abstract painting! The Picasso bug, or Zulu Hud bug

(*Sphaerocoris annulus*), can be found in tropical regions of Africa, such as Nigeria, Tanzania and South Africa. This species is closely related to shield bugs, and measures around eight millimetres in length. Their ornate coloured patterns arise due to pigmented chitin, and they serve as a warning for predators as their bodies contain a variety of toxic chemicals. Like their shield bug cousins, Picasso bugs can release a potent, and noxious odour from holes in their abdomen, when they are threatened. Predators find this odour extremely unpleasant, and will often flee from their prey. The Picasso bug feeds on nectar and other juices from a range of tropical plants. It uses its sharp proboscis to extract the plant's fluids, sucking them up like a straw. The bug lays its eggs underneath leaves and the nymphs feed entirely on flowers, developing into adults by two months of age.

Giant Otter:

The giant otter (*Pteronura brasiliensis*) is the largest species of otter and is one of the Amazon's top predators. They are native to the Pantanal and the Amazon Basin, and grow to nearly two metres in length! They have several aquatic adaptations, including a rudder-like tail, webbed feet and water-resistant fur. Their ears and nostrils are sealable and close before they get into the water.

Giant otters live in family groups consisting of up to ten members. These groups are made up of the parents, along with several generations of their offspring. They aggressively defend their family's territory and all members of the group will mark their home using urine, faeces, loud noises and a scent which is produced from a gland in their anus. They are very vocal animals, and at least twenty-two different vocalisations are used to communicate with each other. These otters hunt alone, or in groups and feed on fish (including piranhas), turtles, large snakes and even caiman! Giant otters are an endangered species and conservationists estimate that there are only five thousand left in the wild. The main perils this animal faces are poaching and habitat destruction.

Philippine Tarsier:

Reaching only ten centimetres in height, the Philippine tarsier (*Carlito syrichta*) is one of the smallest primates on Earth and can fit in the palm of a human hand! There are eighteen species of tarsier and the group has been around for more than forty-five million years. *Carlito syrichta* can be found in various islands in the southern half of the Philippines. The most striking feature of this primate are its huge eyes, which are actually larger than both its stomach and its brain! These eyes are fixed in place in their skull; however, they are able to turn their heads 180 degrees like an owl. Their sensitive eyes allow them to skilfully hunt insects, small lizards and birds during the night.

Philippine tarsiers can leap up to three metres using a specialised ankle bone, which is highly elongated. Females have several pairs of breasts, but most of them are used for offspring to hold onto, with only one set able to produce milk. During mating, the female will mark the male using a scent gland near her mouth. Although they appear cute and cuddly, they are actually very aggressive animals, and males will often fight to the death during territorial disputes. The winner of these fights will even kill the opponent's offspring! Like many species of tarsier, it is endangered, with only five thousand to ten thousand individuals left in the wild. These numbers continue to drop with ongoing forest clearing and illegal capture for the pet trade.

Bearded Vulture:

Bearded vultures (*Gypaetus barbatus*) are huge birds of prey, with a wingspan of almost three metres, and a weight of up to eight kilograms. Also known as the lammergeier or ossifrage (which means 'bone breaker'), the bird makes its nests in the mountains of Africa, Asia and southern Europe. It is the only animal with a diet consisting almost entirely of bones. Its stomach is extremely acidic, allowing it to break down large chunks of the hard substance. It is estimated that as much as ninety percent of the vulture's diet is bone! They scavenge from dead animals, and break their bones by dropping them from great heights onto the rocks below. They can carry animal remains that weigh almost as much as themselves. They also eat turtles, using the same 'drop-and-smash' technique to crack open their thick shells. Live animals such as lizards and rabbits have also been dropped onto rocks to kill them, and they occasionally hunt goats and antelope, scaring them off cliffs so that they plunge to their deaths. The bearded vulture has naturally black and white plumage, but they give their feathers an orange tint by rubbing soil on their bodies, and drinking water rich in minerals. Sadly, the species has become threatened with extinction due to habitat degradation and illegal hunting.

Emperor Newt:

This brightly coloured amphibian is endemic to the Chinese province of Yunnan. The emperor newt, or Mandarin newt (*Tylototriton shanjing*), measures twenty centimetres from head to tail, and has colourful markings on its body, usually orange or red in colour. Large orange bumps are present on their sides, which are filled with poison. They have a bony head and back for added protection. If it is attacked, the Mandarin newt will employ an extraordinary defence mechanism, where it protracts its ribs from the orange warts on its abdomen. As the ribs are extended, they draw out poison from the glands and pierce the attacker's skin. It is a highly toxic animal, containing enough poison to kill around seven thousand mice. Despite its toxicity, it is preyed upon by snakes and raptors, who have evolved a tolerance to the newt's poisonous chemicals. In the breeding season, newts will engage in a 'dance' involving rhythmic, circular movements before mating can occur. The emperor newt is threatened by habitat loss, and over-collection for traditional 'medicine' and the pet trade.

Ocean Sunfish:

The ocean sunfish (*Mola mola*) is the heaviest bony fish in the world. This colossal creature weighs up to 2,300 kilograms and measures a maximum of 3.2 metres from fin to fin! They are as long as they are tall, and have thin, mucus-covered bodies. They can be found in warm waters across the world and are hunted by killer whales, sharks and sea lions. Their main food source is jellyfish, which they capture with their beak-like mouth. As jellyfish are not very nutritious, sunfish have to eat a lot of them, and spend most of their time eating. Over forty different parasites have been recorded living on the sunfish, and it will often breach the surface, so that seagulls and cleaner fish can remove these parasites from its disc-like body.

Female sunfish can release a staggering three hundred million eggs at one time, more than any other vertebrate! They bask in warm waters near the surface, to warm themselves up after diving for long periods. Sunfish are classified as vulnerable, and gillnet fishing is the main reason for their declining population. Another factor in their decline is pollution, as they can suffocate on plastic debris which is mistaken for prey.

Fennec Fox:

The fennec fox (*Vulpes zerda*) is the smallest species of canid, native to the deserts of northern Africa. It has huge ears compared to the rest of its body, which are used to cool themselves down by dissipating heat. These massive ears are also great for sensing animals moving underground, and they will turn their heads from side to side in order to identify the exact location of prey. These adorable foxes eat small birds, mammals, insects and eggs. Adults can be as small as twenty-four centimetres and weigh just a kilogram, smaller than the average house cat! Its unusually large ears can grow to about half the length of its body.

Fennec foxes mate for life, and live in small family groups of about ten individuals, sleeping in long burrows during the day. Thick fur on their feet stops them from being burnt by the extreme heat of the desert sand, and also helps to protect the fox from cold desert nights. They are very agile creatures, and are capable of leaping up to 1.2 metres forward and sixty centimetres into the air in order to evade predators. They can go without water indefinitely, gaining all their moisture from fruits, eggs and leaves. Local populations of fennec foxes are under threat by humans, who hunt them for their fur, and catch them to sell as exotic pets.

Olm:

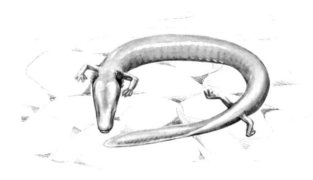

Olms, or human fish (*Proteus anguinus*), are blind amphibians found only in the underwater caves of the Dinaric Alps in southern Europe. They have long, slender bodies which lack pigment, but appear pink in colour due to blood capillaries near the skin's surface. External gills are present on their heads, but adults also possess lungs. They have small, undeveloped limbs and a body length of twenty-five centimetres. Larval features are retained throughout the olm's adult life.

This odd salamander lives in complete darkness, and because of this, it has lost the function of its eyes. However, its hearing and smell are both exceptional, and it relies on these senses to navigate and hunt in its pitch-black environment. Olms prey upon molluscs, crabs and insects, which they swallow whole. They hunt by tracking their prey's chemical cues, sound waves, vibrations and even electric fields! With this impressive set of hunting skills, they have no problem finding food, although they can live without a meal for more than ten years at a time! They have the longest lifespan of any amphibian, living to over one hundred years of age. A rare subspecies of olm exists, which has normal eyes and dark skin. It's called the black olm (*Proteus anguinus parkelj*), and it inhabits warmer waters near the surface. The olm is vulnerable to extinction, and its population has dropped in recent years due to over collection, habitat loss and pollution.

Javan Mouse-Deer:

Measuring a mere forty-five centimetres long, the Javan mouse-deer (*Tragulus javanicus*) is the smallest hoofed animal in the world. Adults are about the same size as rabbits, weighing just one kilogram. They are native to the rainforests of Java, and forage for plants, fungi and insects on the forest floor. They have round bodies and thin legs, and don't grow any horns; instead, males possess long tusks. These tusks are used to defend their territory, and to fight competing males during the mating season. Both sexes mark their territory with a gland on their chin, which releases a smelly substance.

Javan mouse-deer are very shy animals, and make a 'crying' sound when agitated. They can run very quickly at rivals, and beat their hooves on the ground to produce a loud 'drumroll'. They are capable of stamping their feet up to seven times a second in order to make this noise! They are preyed upon by snakes, dogs, birds and crocodiles. Not much is known about the conservation status of the Javan mouse-deer, but it is very likely that the population is decreasing due to human development on their island home.

Greenland Shark:

The Greenland shark (*Somniosus microcephalus*) is the longest-living vertebrate on Earth, reaching an estimated four hundred years of age! Amazingly, it takes about 150 years before the shark reaches adulthood and is able to mate. It inhabits the Arctic and North Atlantic oceans at depths of up to 2,200 metres, and can reach lengths of over six metres and weighs over one thousand kilograms. It is a very slow swimmer, which might be one of the reasons why it can live so long. Their diet consists mainly of fish (including other sharks), seals and dead animals such as moose, polar bears and horses. The shark may sneak up on seals while they sleep, as their slow swimming speed would make it impossible to chase them when they're awake.

The Greenland shark's eyes provide a home to a nasty parasitic copepod (*Ommatokoita elongata*) which permanently latches onto its corneas, producing bioluminescence to lure small organisms which they eat. This results in extreme damage to the eye, but the shark can live without vision due to the deep, dark environments they inhabit. The shark's tissues contain vast quantities of a highly toxic chemical called trimethylamine N-oxide (TMAO). Despite this, humans still eat the animal, and it is considered a delicacy in Iceland. In order to be safe for consumption, the flesh needs to be fermented for months beforehand. The Greenland shark's main threats are hunting and being caught as bycatch. As they take so long to reach maturity, populations face a real struggle to recover.

Honduran White Bat:

Growing to only four centimetres in length, the Honduran white bat (*Ectophylla alba*) is one of the smallest mammals on the planet! They have fuzzy white hair and bright yellow faces – a very rare colouration in bats. A black, membranous structure is present on their heads which shelters them from ultraviolet radiation. This species lives in the thick forests of Central America, from Honduras to western Panama.

Also known as the tent-making bat, these creatures construct a shelter out of leaves, which they cut with their teeth and fold down to create a sort of tent. They sleep in these shelters during the day and leave at night to forage for fruit. When sunlight filters through the leaves of their shelter, and onto their bodies, the bat's white fur appears to glow green. This acts as camouflage, making them harder to spot against the surrounding foliage. If a predator brushes past the bats' tent, they will be woken up by the vibrations and fly off to hide in a secondary shelter. They normally live in small groups of about six individuals, which is made up of a male and a group of females that he mates with, called a harem. Although, sometimes they do nest on their own. Habitat loss is a major problem for the survival of the species, since their nesting requirements are so specific. For this reason, they are deemed a threatened species.

Assassin Bug:

Assassin bugs (*Reduviidae*) are a family of predatory insects that can be found all over the world. These formidable bugs have a sharp, curved mouthpart which is used to stab prey and deliver a toxic saliva. This deadly substance breaks down the soft tissue inside the body of its prey, liquefying it. The digested insides are then extracted via the proboscis until just the dry shell of the victim is left. Some assassin bugs bite humans in soft areas such as the eyes and mouth to extract blood. These are known as kissing bugs, and they can spread fatal diseases. Other species squirt venom which can result in short-term blindness in humans.

Assassin bugs are masters of disguise, with some species, such as the masked hunter (*Reduvius personatus*), covering themselves in dirt and dust to blend into their surroundings. *Stenolemus bituberus* is an assassin bug from Australia that specialises in hunting spiders, which it achieves by mimicking prey caught in the spider's web. They pluck the threads of the web, luring the spider out before quickly striking and injecting their lethal saliva. Feather-legged bugs (*Ptilocnemus lemur*) hunt ants with a specialised glandular outgrowth called a trichome. This organ lures prey with a chemical, and then paralyses them when they come into contact with it. Some species will even decorate their bodies with the corpses of their prey, and are sometimes seen with dozens of ants placed on their backs! This provides camouflage, allowing the bug to hunt its way through ant colonies undetected.

Barreleye Fish:

The barreleye, or spookfish (*Macropinna microstoma*), is a peculiar deep-sea fish with unique, tube-like eyes and a transparent head! They live mainly in the waters of California and the north Pacific, at depths of six hundred to eight hundred metres. This fish can rotate its eyes (which are located inside its fluid-filled head) to view potential prey above, or move them to look forward when swimming or feeding. These fish inhabit near pitch-black waters, so they have extremely sensitive eyes that pick up the faintest silhouettes cast by prey overhead. They are known to eat small fish, crustaceans and jellyfish, although their large digestive systems suggest that they have a much broader diet. The barreleye fish has a very specific hunting method, where it floats motionless waiting for prey. In this position, it aims its eyes upward. When prey is detected, they turn their eyes forward and swim up ready to catch their meal. They also steal food that siphonophores capture in their long, stinging tentacles. The barreleye's liquid-filled head protects their eyes from the siphonophores' dangerous stinging cells. Some species of barreleye have bioluminescent organs, which might act as camouflage, by breaking up the fish's silhouette.

Mary River Turtle:

The Mary River turtle (*Elusor macrurus*) or 'punk rock turtle' as it is also known, is an endangered species that is found only in the Mary River in Queensland, Australia. Its shell measures up to fifty centimetres, and it feeds mainly on algae. Although it normally breathes out of the water, it can absorb oxygen through a gill-like organ near its anus, in a process called cloacal ventilation. This method of breathing allows the turtle to remain underwater for days without surfacing.

The Mary River turtle possesses four feeling tentacles under its chin called barbels, and a unique bony tail that can grow to almost the length of its shell. Its barbels help it find prey, such as aquatic insects and molluscs that hide in sandy riverbeds. It is often spotted with algae growing on its shell or head, which provides the animal with an effective disguise. Since 1970, the total number of Mary River turtles has dropped by ninety-five percent due to habitat loss, water degradation and the collection of babies in the 1970s for the pet trade. It is now among the twenty-five most endangered turtle species in the world.

Pangolin:

Pangolins are unique, as they are the only group of mammals that possess scales. There are eight different types of pangolin, and they live in Africa and Asia. The tree pangolin *(Phataginus tricuspis)* is one of the smallest, measuring forty centimetres in length. They live in central

African rainforests and shelter in hollowed-out tree trunks. When in danger, they curl into a ball, protecting their soft tissues with their scaly armour. A noxious odour can also be emitted by the pangolin from scent glands near its anus, which keeps predators at bay. It feeds mostly on ants and collects them using its sticky tongue which is seventy centimetres in length! Pangolins also swallow stones, which help to break down food in their stomach, as they lack the teeth to crush their prey. Armoured scales also protect these creatures from ant bites, as do their thick eyelids. Muscles on their ears and nostrils enable these openings to be firmly closed when ants are crawling nearby.

Baby pangolins have soft scales, which harden after a few days. Mothers carry them on their tails and will tuck them safely under their bellies at any sign of danger. All species of pangolin are threatened with extinction, and they are the most trafficked mammal on Earth. Over the last ten years, more than a million of these animals have been taken from the wild. Their main threats are hunting for bush meat and Chinese traditional 'medicine', along with habitat loss.

Peacock Spider:

The peacock spider (*Maratus volans*) is a tiny jumping spider endemic to Australia. They are only five millimetres long, and males have brightly coloured flaps on their abdomens. These intricately patterned flaps serve to attract mates, and the ones with the brightest patterns have a better chance of mating. But this isn't the only way in which males woo the ladies; the spider also performs a 'dance' where he raises his iridescent flaps, and puts his two back legs in the air. He then waves his legs around, shakes his abdomen, and raises and lowers the flap. The male will also clap his back legs together to try and get attention. If the desired female is not impressed by the dance moves, she will try to kill and eat him! Even if the lady spider is receptive and mating does occur, the male isn't necessarily safe. Females will sometimes cannibalise males after fertilisation. Over seventy species of peacock spider have been discovered, and each species has a unique pattern on their back, with different colours and shapes. Females and young spiders lack these colourful abdomens.

Mantis Shrimp:

There are over four hundred species of mantis shrimp (*Stomatopoda*), which average ten centimetres in length and reside in shallow, tropical seas. They are truly bizarre creatures, with their vibrantly coloured bodies, powerful spearing or smashing claws, and the most intricate visual system in the animal kingdom. They have a staggering sixteen different types of colour-receptive cone cells in their eyes (we have just three, and they allow us to see all the colours we know). The eyes of the mantis shrimp are found at the end of stalks, and can move around independently from each other.

Their diet consists of other shrimp and fish, and they have two main hunting techniques, depending on the species. Some lurk on the seafloor, waiting for prey to swim by, before impaling them with elongated, dagger-like pincers. Others shatter their prey with club-shaped claws, striking with the same speed as a .22-caliber bullet! The shrimp's punch is so powerful that it can even break aquarium glass. For a split second after striking, the shrimp's punch creates air bubbles and raises the temperature of the surrounding water to thousands of degrees! When these air bubbles collapse, they create shockwaves that can kill prey, even if the initial impact does not. This force can crack even the hardest of shells, allowing the mantis shrimp to feed on the soft tissue of its victims.

Southern Marsupial Mole:

The southern marsupial mole (*Notoryctes typhlops*) is a rare, burrowing marsupial from the deserts of south-western Australia. They are not related to moles, but have independently evolved several similar features that make them well-suited to a life underground. Just like placental moles, they have a tubular body, silky fur, strong front limbs, and tiny eyes and ears. The remarkable similarities between moles and marsupial moles is an example of convergent evolution. Marsupial moles also appear almost identical to golden moles (*Chrysochloridae*) – a group of subterranean mammals from Africa that are also unrelated to true moles.

Marsupial moles eat insects, small reptiles and eggs. Huge, spade-shaped claws are located at the front of its body, which help to rapidly scoop away soil. They require very little oxygen to survive, breathing the air that flows through grains of sand. Like all marsupials, they raise their young in a pouch, but theirs faces backwards to stop it from filling with dirt. Introduced predators and altered grazing and fire regimes are their main threats, although little is known about their conservation status due to the animal's mysterious nature.

Bone-Eating Snot Flower:

The bone-eating snot flower (*Osedax mucofloris*) is a unique polychaete found in the deep sea. They are about two centimetres long and feed on the bones of whales that sink to the seafloor after death. Completely lacking a mouth or stomach, they only eat by absorbing nutrients that symbiotic bacteria digest for them. They drill through the whale's bones by secreting acids, so they can reach the nutritious lipids contained inside the marrow. Their feathery appendages extract oxygen from the water like fish gills and when they are feeding, they poke out of the bone, and look like flowers.

Males are microscopic and never develop; instead, they live inside the female, continuously releasing sperm to fertilise her eggs. A single female can have over one hundred males living inside her! Females have a thick layer of mucus surrounding their 'trunks' which houses the males. They are able to disperse their larvae over huge distances, and the environment determines which sex they develop into. If the larvae land near fresh whale carcasses, they will grow in size and become females. If the remains are already occupied by females, they will instead develop into males and are taken up by the opposite sex. The hunting of whales may be a threat to this species, as it reduces their already scarce food supply.

Kagu:

Native to the island of New Caledonia is a unique bird called the kagu (*Rhynochetos jubatus*). It lives in mountainous forests, and adults measure fifty-five centimetres in height. It is a near-flightless bird that hunts insects and lizards from the forest floor, and is decorated with a beautiful crest, white plumage and bright red eyes. The bird's feathers produce a powder that keeps them insulated and clean. Despite being flightless, the kagu has large wings. These aid in balance whilst running, and also act as a defence mechanism, scaring away predators from their chicks by flapping them frantically.

When hunting, the kagu will wait patiently for hours at a time. They stand on one foot and wait for insects to get close, before snapping them up very quickly. They also dig for prey which they impale with their sharp beak. Kagus pair for life, and give birth to one chick every year. Both sexes help to incubate the egg and raise their offspring, taking turns guarding the nest. Chicks will stay with their parents for up to six years, and help to guard their family's territory. They are the only bird to have a structure called 'nasal corns' on their beak. These help to prevent soil from entering the nostrils whilst digging. Kagus evolved on an island with very few natural predators, but they have now become endangered via predation from introduced cats and dogs. Their eggs are also easy prey for invasive rats.

Golden Snub-Nosed Monkey:

The endangered golden snub-nosed monkey (*Rhinopithecus roxellana*) lives in very secluded areas of central China. They can be found in high mountain forests in large groups of up to six hundred members. Males reach seventy centimetres in height and females are shorter, standing at fifty centimetres. They have orangey-brown fur and a blue face, but the most noticeable feature of this primate is its oddly shaped stump of a nose. Their habitat can become extremely cold in the winter, so a short nose is beneficial as it prevents frostbite (they also have thick fur covering their hands like mittens). However, the shape of their nose does have its disadvantages. When it rains, water runs down their face, and into their nostrils, making them sneeze. For this reason, they hide under trees during rain showers. Males have a brighter coat, and the colours become more vivid as they grow older.

The golden snub-nosed monkey spends ninety-seven percent of its time in the trees: grazing, mating and sleeping there. Their diet changes a lot during the year. In the summer, they eat leaves, insects and fruit, and in the winter, they eat mostly tree bark and pine needles. Lichen forms a large part of their diet year-round. For mating to take place, the female must initiate it, and she does so by approaching the male and flashing her genitals. Unfortunately, this species has lost a lot of its habitat in recent years and it is hunted by humans for fur and meat.

Blue-Footed Booby:

The blue-footed booby (*Sula nebouxii*) is a magnificent bird from the tropical and subtropical waters of the Pacific. They are ninety centimetres long and their wings measure 1.5 metres outstretched. Males have distinctive blue feet, which help to attract mates. When a female selects a male, she will choose the one with the most colourful feet, as this is a sign of good health and fertility. During the breeding season, males will give females a small gift such as a twig or rock, before engaging in an unusual mating display. This involves the male lifting his head up to the sky, and opening its wings wide, before lifting his feet up and down in a sort of strut. The purpose of this mating dance is to show off the feet, and if the female is sufficiently impressed, they will mate for life.

Males gain their blue pigment by eating lots of fresh fish, and when their food supply is reduced, the colour of their feet fades. Blue-footed boobies also use their feet to incubate their eggs – a task carried out by both males and females. When the eggs hatch, some chicks may be a lot bigger than their siblings, and when food is scarce, the smaller chick will be eaten by its brothers and sisters. Although it is not classed as endangered, the blue-footed booby has suffered a slow population decline because of breeding problems related to a drop in the numbers of fish (especially sardines).

Saiga:

The saiga (*Saiga tatarica*) is a rare antelope native to the grasslands and savannahs of central Asia. It is small for an antelope, measuring eighty centimetres at the shoulder (about the same size as a sheep). It has straight, ringed horns that can reach lengths of forty centimetres. Its oversized nose is an adaptation to the extremes of its desert environment. This weird-shaped snout filters out dust from inhaled air, and cools the animal's blood in the summer. It also warms the winter air before it reaches the lungs, keeping the antelope's internal body temperature stable.

Saigas once formed some of the largest herds on the planet, grouping together in the tens of thousands to migrate. However, the wild population of saigas has dropped by a staggering ninety-five percent over the past fifteen years. They are now critically endangered, and on the verge of extinction. The main reason for this steep fall in numbers is poaching for meat and horns, which are used in traditional Chinese 'medicine'. In addition, their population has been decimated over the last few years by a fatal bacterium called *Pasteurella multocida*. This microorganism usually lives peacefully inside the antelopes, posing no threat to them, but recent extreme weather somehow mutated it into a deadly pathogen. This phenomenon has an extremely high death rate and can wipe out whole herds by shutting down vital organs and causing blood poisoning. Some areas have experienced a slow recovery of saiga populations due to the hard work of organisations like the Saiga Conservation Alliance.

Pacific Hagfish:

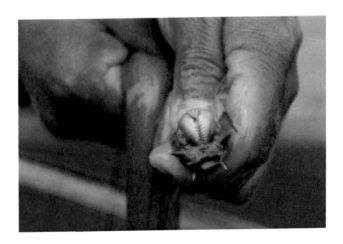

Pacific hagfish (*Eptatretus stoutii*) are eel-like fish that have remained relatively unchanged for three hundred million years. They can be found on the seafloor of the Pacific Ocean, between eighteen and nine hundred metres deep. Growing to over sixty centimetres long, hagfish are the only animal with a skull but no backbone. They have five hearts, no eyes, no stomach and no jaws, and are able to absorb nutrients through their skin! They hunt polychaetes, crabs and small fish from the seafloor. They also feed off dead, dying or injured fish, often forcing their way inside the animal through the anus or mouth. Once inside, they feast upon the fish's internal organs. Hagfish are also fond of dead whales, and are usually the first animals spotted on a whale carcass.

When threatened, the hagfish has the ability to produce vast amounts of slime almost instantly, which confuses and repulses predators as it tastes so bad. This slime can also enter the gills of predatory fish, preventing them from breathing. If the slime doesn't manage to deter the attacker, hagfish can tie themselves in a knot to escape. Hagfish create the sticky substance by releasing proteins from glands on their skin, which turns into a thick slime and expands rapidly when it comes into contact with saltwater. The main threat to the hagfish is fishing for its skin.

Wolverine:

Wolverines (*Gulo gulo*) look like a cross between a bear and a skunk, but in fact, they are neither. They actually belong to the weasel family and are the largest species in this group. They measure over a metre in length, and weigh up to thirty-two kilograms. They inhabit colder regions of northern Asia, Europe and North America.

Wolverines are very aggressive and can kill animals much larger than themselves, hunting caribou, moose and even bison! Despite their immense killing potential, they prefer to scavenge meat and follow the trail of wolf packs, so they can devour their leftovers. They eat almost anything they come across, including seeds, berries and roots. Their strong jaws can crush bone and teeth, and they also hunt porcupines, even swallowing their spines! The animal consumes a tremendous amount of food at a time, which has led to them being nicknamed 'gluttons'. When they can't fit anything else in their stomachs, they will store excess food in the snow, using it as a refrigerator. Wolverines are not endangered, although their numbers have fallen recently due to hunting. Climate change may also pose a threat to the species in the future.

Gharial:

This bizarre creature is one of the largest species of crocodilian, growing to an amazing 6.25 metres long! It is called the gharial (*Gavialis gangeticus*), and is found in northern India, Pakistan and Myanmar. Compared to its crocodilian relatives, it has an extremely narrow snout, and males have a huge bump on their nose which is used to attract mates. Adults have a diet made up entirely of fish, and their thin, spear-like mouth can be whipped through the water quickly to catch them, with little water resistance. Their legs are quite weak and they are unable to walk on land. Instead, they must slide around to travel out of the water.

The gharial is a critically endangered species, with an estimated 235 animals left in the wild. In the 1970s, it was at the very brink of extinction, but a breeding programme was set up which saved the species, by reintroducing many gharials into the wild. However, the fate of the gharial is still uncertain as habitat loss, fishing and hunting continue to affect the population. The animal's eggs and snout are used in traditional 'medicine' and overfishing is destroying their food source.

Pom Pom Crab:

Pom pom crabs, or boxer crabs (*Lybia edmondsoni*) have a fascinating symbiotic relationship with stinging anemones. They keep these anemones on their claws and use them to fight off attackers by waving their claws at them, stinging them into submission. The anemones also collect food floating by, which sticks to their tentacles, and is scraped off and consumed by the crab. These living claw accessories may even be used to stun and catch prey! The anemones benefit from this arrangement too, as they can eat scraps of food leftover by the crab, and are mobile so they can extract more food from the water.

These living appendages are extremely valuable to the pom pom crab, and they often fight over them. Those without anemones will try and steal one from another crab, and are often successful. If a crab loses one of its anemones, it will rip the other one in half, creating a clone that will regenerate and grow into a fully sized adult. The crab's claws are very small, and are only used to carry the anemones. The claws are covered with lots of tiny hooks to keep the anemones in place. To stop their 'pom poms' from growing too large to manage, they will prune them by biting pieces off of them, and they will also limit their food supply. It is not known how, or where the crabs get their anemones, as they have not been found living anywhere other than on a crab claw. Pom pom crabs are native to the coral reefs of Hawaii, and are very small, measuring just a centimetre long.

Lesser Egyptian Jerboa:

The lesser Egyptian jerboa (*Jaculus jaculus*) is a small rodent that lives in North Africa and the Middle East, and measures ten centimetres in length. It moves around by jumping, and its powerful, elongated hind legs allow the creature to leap up to three metres! The jerboa's tail is longer than the rest of its body, and aids with balance when jumping. This kangaroo-like rodent has been recorded travelling over ten kilometres per day in the search for food, which includes insects, plant matter and fungi. It doesn't need to drink, as it receives sufficient water by eating plant material. It forages during the night, and hides in tunnels throughout the day, safe from predators and the heat of the sun. Jerboas cover the entrance to these tunnels in summer to keep their dens cool, and also construct an 'emergency exit' just below the main entrance to quickly escape if predators break in. They are hunted by owls, foxes and snakes, and can travel at speeds of twenty-four kilometres per hour (fifteen miles per hour) when chased.

Before copulation can take place, the jerboa must perform a very unique mating ritual. First, the male positions himself next to a female, upright on his back legs. Then he will repeatedly slap the female with his front paws, enticing her to mate with him. As they have a very large range, the lesser Egyptian jerboa as a species is not endangered. However, populations are at risk in Syria and Jordan because they are hunted for meat and used as bait for falcons.

Marine Iguana:

Marine iguanas (*Amblyrhynchus cristatus*) live exclusively on the Galapagos Islands and measure up to a metre in length. When Charles Darwin visited the islands in 1835, he described the iguanas as 'disgusting clumsy lizards' and called them 'imps of darkness'. Marine iguanas are herbivores, and spend up to an hour foraging underwater, feeding entirely on algae and seaweed. The largest males have been observed diving to twenty metres! Unique among lizards, they are the only marine lizards alive today. Their sharp teeth and flat faces allow them to scrape off algae from rocks, and they have special glands in their nose to remove salt from their blood. Salt is expelled in a similar way to sneezing, and often builds up, encrusting on the top of their heads.

After diving for food, marine iguanas must warm up by basking in the sun, and their black skin speeds up the process as it absorbs heat. They bask in enormous groups of over a thousand, and are unable to move properly until their body temperature has returned to normal. Crabs patrol these sunbathing groups and pick off and eat the iguanas' dead skin. Hatchlings eat the faeces of adult iguanas to gain the bacteria required to digest algae. It is a threatened species, with climate change potentially becoming a huge problem in the future. Global warming can increase the frequency of an extreme weather event known as 'El Niño', which warms the water around the islands and prevents algae (their main food source) from growing.

Lowland Streaked Tenrec:

Lowland streaked tenrecs (*Hemicentetes semispinosus*) can be found in the tropical rainforests of eastern Madagascar and measure up to sixteen centimetres. They are similar in appearance to hedgehogs or shrews, but have independently evolved these features and are not closely related to either. They have a collection of quills on their bodies, which are either barbed, or detachable. These spikes come in handy when the tenrec is faced with a predator. When threatened, it will jerk its head violently, piercing the paws, or nose of the attacker with its quills. The commotion caused by this defence mechanism gives the creature time to run away. Remarkably, their quills also function as a way of communicating with each other. This is achieved by vibrating their bodies, which rattles the quills together, resulting in a low-pitched noise. This type of sound production is called stridulation, and is normally used by snakes and insects.

Lowland streaked tenrecs live underground in family groups of up to twenty members. Their main food source is earthworms, which they dig up with their long snouts. Although the species is not currently threatened, deforestation continues on a large scale in Madagascar and this may impact their habitat in the future.

Matschie's Tree Kangaroo

Tree kangaroos are the arboreal cousins of kangaroos, native to New Guinea and Australia. They have large grip-pads on their paws, curved claws for climbing, and huge tails for balancing in the treetops. They are not very fast or agile on the ground, but in the trees, they are nimble and graceful. These marsupials can hop up tree trunks at great speeds, and are able to jump eighteen metres to the ground without being harmed. They have extremely powerful back legs that allow them to propel themselves an incredible nine metres! Matschie's tree kangaroo (*Dendrolagus matschiei*) is one of the largest species at eighty centimetres in length, and eleven kilograms in weight. It is endemic to the Huon Peninsula of Papua New Guinea, and like most tree kangaroos, it is listed as endangered. It has thick, golden-brown fur and a large tail which is about the same size as its body. Like ground kangaroos, they are unable to sweat. Instead, they lick themselves all over to cool down by evaporation. This species eats for just one or two hours a day, foraging for leaves, insects and fruit. They initiate mating by touching each other's noses and sex can last for up to an hour. The population of Matschie's tree kangaroo has fallen because of deforestation, hunting and oil drilling.

Lilac-Breasted Roller:

The lilac-breasted roller (*Coracias caudatus*) can be found throughout sub-Saharan Africa and the Arabian Peninsula, and grows to thirty centimetres in height. They have a magnificent plumage containing a vast array of colours such as blue, white, turquoise, brown, green and of course, lilac. Unlike most birds, these bright colours are present in both sexes.

Lilac-breasted rollers spend most of their time perched on tall branches looking out for prey. They eat insects, small mammals, lizards, frogs and even other birds. They are highly aggressive in nature, and will violently thrash prey around and batter it on the floor to stun it, before swallowing it whole. Sometimes these beatings will result in the prey being dismembered! When a bushfire breaks out, the lilac-breasted roller is one of the first animals on the scene, ready to pick off easy prey that is fleeing from the fire. They are named 'rollers' because of their dramatic courtship displays which involve a rapid dive from a tremendous height. Whilst diving, the bird will tilt its body from side to side in a 'rolling' motion and call loudly.

Golden Tortoise Beetle:

This magnificent insect is called the golden tortoise beetle or goldbug (*Charidotella sexpunctata*), and it can be found in North and South America. It is only five millimetres in length, and feeds on sweet potato plants and their related species. This beetle has a transparent wing case, and a metallic-looking shell which varies in colour from gold to brown or red. The tortoise beetle can also change colour whilst mating, and when it's agitated. This colour change is the result of fluid flowing through channels on its exoskeleton. When it's disturbed, the beetle will dry out its water channels and this changes the colour of the shell to red.

Larvae of this species collect their shed skins and their faeces, to form a protective cover to hide from predators. This is known as a 'faecal shield' and is attached to an organ called the anal fork. This faecal shield is moveable, and is a very effective protection against small predators, such as ants.

Pyrenean Desman:

Found in the mountain streams of northern Spain and Portugal is the bizarre Pyrenean desman (*Galemys pyrenaicus*). They are aquatic mammals that are closely related to moles. They have a body length of sixteen centimetres, and their tails measure roughly the same size. The desman possesses webbed back feet and a flattened, rudder-like tail for swimming. Valves are present on their ears and nostrils to prevent water getting in. The creature has poor eyesight, but its highly sensitive nose is very effective at sensing prey in the murky waters. During the night, they hunt shrimp, snails and insect larvae by probing their nose into mud and crevices. They may also use echolocation to navigate and detect prey, by hitting the surface of the water with their tails and producing sound. Scent glands on their bodies release a musky smell which marks their territory. They reside in pairs, and are very aggressive to intruders, often fighting to the death to defend their home. The Pyrenean desman is vulnerable to water pollution and habitat degradation from the construction of hydroelectric dams.

Texas Horned Lizard:

Texas horned lizards (*Phrynosoma cornutum*) are small reptiles that range from Colorado to northern Mexico. They feed almost exclusively on ants, and have a variety of techniques to avoid being eaten by predators. The colours on their bodies match their surroundings, and large spikes composed of modified scales make them hard to pick up. They can also expand their bodies a bit like a puffer fish to scare off attackers. If the lizard is spotted by a wolf or dog, it will run in small bursts, and stop suddenly to throw them off. If these defence mechanisms don't work, they press their head and body to the ground, making themselves harder to pick up. However, the horned lizard's most remarkable defence is its ability to shoot blood out of its eyes! It does this by increasing the pressure in its head, and rupturing blood vessels in its eyes, making a jet of blood squirt out as far as 1.5 metres. Up to a third of its blood volume can be expelled from its eyes whilst defending itself. This confuses predators, and also tastes disgusting as the blood is filled with nasty chemicals. Apparently, wolves and dogs react worse to this method of self-defence. In the last few decades, the population of Texas horned lizards has declined rapidly, and about half of its natural range has been lost.

Suriname Toad:

The Suriname toad (*Pipa pipa*) is native to the tropics of South America, and has a flat body that resembles a dried leaf. They measure up to twenty centimetres long, and produce sound by snapping a special bone in their mouth. They have no tongue or teeth, and have tiny eyes. These frogs hunt fish by suction feeding, and lurk at the bottom of freshwater rivers, sensing prey with their long, unwebbed fingers.

During mating, the male grasps the female's waist in a position known as the amplexus. They will then somersault in the water, and at this point, the female will lay eggs onto the male's belly. The male will fertilise these eggs and then embed them into the skin on the female's back! This process can take up to twenty-four hours to complete, with up to one hundred eggs being implanted into the female's skin. Over time, the eggs move deeper into their mother's back, and skin grows over them for protection. Each egg is now in a kind of 'pocket' and they will develop there until it is time to hatch. The tadpole stage actually occurs inside these pockets and after some weeks, the offspring burst out of their mother's skin, emerging as small, but fully developed toads.

Bobbit Worm:

The bobbit worm (*Eunice aphroditois*) is a giant polychaete worm that can be found on the seafloor between ten and forty metres deep. They live in warm waters all around the world, and can reach an incredible three metres in length, with some reports of them growing to six metres! The worm's body is brown or red, but it also exhibits iridescence, and has five antennae on the front of its head to sense prey. They bury themselves in the seafloor with only their heads exposed, ready to ambush fish and smaller worms. When they detect prey nearby, they strike at the animal with a great force, grabbing them with their strange mouth part called the pharynx. The victim is then dragged to its doom, where it is injected with venom that either stuns or kills it. The worm's attack is so vicious that it can sometimes slice its prey in half!

A bobbit worm accidently made its way into an aquarium in Cornwall, and caused massive destruction to the organisms in one of their tanks. Coral were found cut in half and fish were missing and injured. When they started dismantling the tank, they discovered the culprit: a metre-long bobbit worm. They named it Barry and moved it into its own tank.

Hooded Seal:

Hooded seals (*Cystophora cristata*) are named after their peculiar inflatable nasal sacs, which puff up into a huge, bulbous structure on the top of their heads. This display can be expanded further by pumping an additional sac through one nostril, whilst the other nostril is shut off with a valve. This produces a secondary inflatable structure which looks like a gigantic pink balloon. Only males possess these strange organs, which are used to scare off competing males and to impress females during the breeding season. They are very aggressive animals; however, most confrontations between males are resolved with the use of the nasal balloon. Large balloons signal strength, so the seal with the smaller balloon will usually retreat in search of another female. If the balloons are of equal size, a fight will ensue. This involves a series of shoving, head-butting and biting, and can result in serious injury.

Male hooded seals have a body length of up to three metres and weigh four hundred kilograms. They live in the cold waters of the North Atlantic and eat squid and fish, diving up to a thousand metres to hunt. Baby seals measure a metre long at birth, and are highly developed. They only breastfeed for four days, but during this time they will double in size! This is the shortest lactation period of any mammal. Hooded seals are classed as vulnerable, and are hunted by humans and accidentally caught in fishing nets.

Sword-Billed Hummingbird:

The sword-billed hummingbird (*Ensifera ensifera*) occurs naturally in the high montane forests of South America. It is the only bird in the world where its beak and tongue are longer than the rest of its body! The hummingbird has to be extra careful when landing due to this heavy structure. To avoid falling over, it must point its bill upward to balance with the rest of its body. It also has to groom itself with its feet, as its beak is far too long to be of any use in preening.

The sword-billed hummingbird has a body length of eight centimetres, whilst its bill reaches over ten! This remarkable beak has evolved so that it can feed on the nectar of the passion flower (*Passiflora mixta*), which is hidden away at the bottom of deep, tubular corollas. This hummingbird is a valuable pollinator, and is the only species that is able to pollinate these slender plants. The female lays two eggs, and raises them herself, while the male defends their territory. They feed their young by shoving food down their throats, placing it directly into the stomach using their elongated bill. Its scientific name, *ensifera*, translates to 'sword-wielder'.

Silky Anteater:

The silky anteater (*Cyclopes didactylus*) is the smallest species of anteater, with a body length of just twenty centimetres. They weigh around three hundred grams, and are native to Central and South America, from Mexico down to Bolivia. Their tail is very flexible, and is used to grip onto tree branches. Curved claws also help the anteater climb trees, and these appendages are very large compared to the rest of its body. Their diet consists mainly of ants, but they also eat small beetles and the occasional fruit. They emerge at night to forage, and can eat over five thousand ants in one day!

Silky anteaters sleep inside hollowed-out trees throughout the day, hiding away from predators. Most of their time is spent in silk cotton trees and their soft, yellow fur resembles the seedpods of these trees, which acts as a camouflage. If threatened, they will produce a harsh scream and will stand on their back legs, using their sharp claws to strike at their attacker. Their main predators are hawks and harpy eagles, which pluck them from the trees. Both males and females care for their offspring, and they feed them regurgitated ants. The male occasionally carries his young on his back. This species has a stable population and a wide distribution; therefore, it is not regarded as endangered.

Chinese Giant Salamander:

The largest amphibian in the world – the Chinese giant salamander (*Andrias davidianus*) – measures almost two metres in length! It is native to southern China, but has also been introduced to parts of Taiwan and Japan. They live in murky rivers and eat insects, fish, frogs, crabs and even other salamanders. They are entirely aquatic and never have to leave the water. They have a large head and tiny eyes, and their skin is black or dark brown, with lots of blotches and wrinkles. Oxygen is absorbed through the skin, and the wrinkles help with gas exchange by increasing the body's surface area.

Chinese giant salamanders hunt using their heightened senses of touch and smell. Males fight each other for breeding territory, and these fights sometimes result in death. Females lay up to five hundred eggs in a cave, or crevice, and the male fertilises them afterwards. He will then guard the eggs for fifty days until they hatch and he will protect them from predators during this time. After hatching, they look like miniature adults, and are just three centimetres long. To fend off predators, giant salamanders will excrete a sticky, white substance from their bodies. They have a long lifespan, reaching over sixty years of age. Chinese giant salamanders are a critically endangered species and over eighty percent of their population has been lost in the last sixty years. The reasons for the decline include hunting for food and traditional Chinese 'medicine', habitat loss and pollution.

Vampire Squid:

Vampire squid (*Vampyroteuthis infernalis*) live in deep, tropical waters from three hundred to three thousand metres down. They grow to thirty centimetres long and have soft bodies that are black or dark red in colour. These squid have red eyes and webbed tentacles, with multiple rows of spiny, tooth-like structures on the inside. Its Latin name literally translates to 'vampire squid from hell'. Their eyes measure 2.5 centimetres in diameter, which means they have the largest eye-to-body ratio in the animal kingdom. Fins can be found on their heads, which look like ears, and they beat them to move around. They are very fast swimmers, propelling themselves through the ocean at two body lengths per second.

When faced with a predator, the vampire squid curls its webbed tentacles over itself like a cloak, effectively turning itself inside out! In this position, its menacing-looking spines are exposed, scaring predators away. A secondary defence mechanism is employed by the squid as a last resort, and involves light-emitting organs called photophores, which are located all over its body. They will illuminate these photophores at the tips of their tentacles, and wave them around wildly. This confuses predators, and makes it very difficult for them to locate the exact position of the squid. They will then release a cloud of mucus at the attacker, containing luminescent particles which causes further distraction, and allows the squid to get away.

Tuatara:

Tuataras (*Sphenodon punctatus*) are the sole surviving species of an ancient group of reptiles that roamed the Earth over two hundred million years ago. They reside on several islands off the coast of New Zealand, although they were once widespread on the mainland. They look like lizards, but are only distantly related to them. Tuataras are brown or green in colour can grow to eighty centimetres. They have a 'third eye' located under the skin on the top of their head which is responsive to light, and is composed of a retina and lens. This organ might be used to monitor day and night cycles, and to help with thermoregulation, although its exact purpose is unclear. The 'eye' is only visible in hatchlings, when it's covered in a semi-transparent membrane.

Tuataras develop very slowly, and have a lifespan of over one hundred years! They lay their eggs every four to nine years, and their incubation period is extremely long for a reptile, only hatching after sixteen months. Adults live in burrows and sometimes share these nests with seabirds. The birds' droppings attract insects that the tuataras eat, and they will occasionally eat the eggs and chicks of their poor cohabitants. The population of tuataras is at risk by the introduction of rats into their island habitats, which is the same factor that caused their demise on the mainland.

Glasswinged Butterfly:

The glasswinged butterfly, or glasswing (*Greta oto*), is a gorgeous insect that can be found in Central and South America, and has a wingspan of six centimetres. It is adorned with magnificent wings that are almost completely transparent! The reason for this is that the wing tissue reflects barely any light, allowing it to pass straight through. These wings also have very low light absorption and scattering rates. The butterfly's see-through wings have evolved as a means to avoid predation, making them harder to spot. Birds find it especially difficult to track the glasswing's movement during flight. It also decreases their shadow, reducing their chances of being detected by land-based predators.

Compared to other butterflies, the glasswing is able to migrate enormous distances, flying, on average, twenty kilometres per day. During the breeding season, males group together and release pheromones to attract females. Caterpillars of this species are poisonous, and they gain their toxicity by feeding on Cestrum plants. Adults are also poisonous, and feed on the nectar of toxic flowers. The chemicals in the nectar of these flowers are particularly unpleasant for birds.

Tentacled Snake:

The tentacled snake (*Erpeton tentaculatum*) is an unusual aquatic snake endemic to Thailand, Cambodia and Vietnam. They inhabit slow moving, shallow rivers and lakes, and live underwater their whole lives. They can hold their breath for thirty minutes, which allows them to hunt for long periods without having to move. The tentacled snake is fairly small, with a maximum body length of ninety centimetres. It has two tube-like appendages on the front of its face, which function as sensors to locate prey. It feeds almost exclusively on fish and has a unique strategy to catch them. It positions its body into a J shape underwater and supports itself by grasping onto a rock or branch with its tail. It will stay in this position until a fish approaches. Then the snake jolts its lower body, which scares the fish, tricking it into swimming in the direction of the snake's mouth. It predicts exactly where the fish will swim to, and moves its head to that specific location, grabbing the fish in its mouth. The tentacled snake is able to hunt in complete darkness, using its sensory tentacles to detect fish (a feature that is not found in any other snake). They also have venom, which contains chemicals that are highly potent to fish. They make use of algae, which grows all over their bodies, allowing them to blend in to their surroundings. Hunting has caused a drop in tentacled snake populations in some areas of Cambodia, although the population as a whole is stable.

Black Dragonfish:

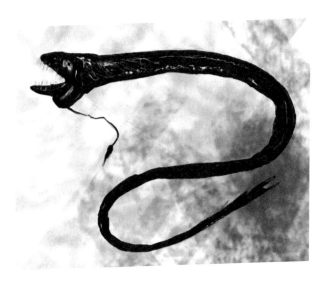

Black dragonfish (*Idiacanthus atlanticus*) are slender fish that can be found in deep, tropical oceans up to two thousand metres from the surface. Females reach forty centimetres in length, dwarfing the males that measure only five centimetres. They have black skin and deadly fang-like teeth. They are bioluminescent, but don't use their light to attract prey, as most other fish can't see it. Instead, they emit a low wavelength light that is close to infrared, and use it to locate prey, without being detected. As well as being much larger, females have lots of features that are unique to their sex, such as a long barbel (a fleshy projection on their mouth), pelvic fins and canines. Males have extremely large testicles that take up a lot of room in their bodies. They also have no digestive system, and their sole purpose is to mate with the female. Notable differences between males and females of a certain species is known as 'sexual dimorphism'.

Black dragonfish feed on other fish and flash with bioluminescence when threatened. Larvae of this species are transparent, and their eyes are positioned at the end of long, thin stalks that can measure up to twenty percent of their body length! The larvae's eyes gradually retreat into the skull as they get older, and their skin gains pigment.

Tiger Quoll:

The tiger quoll, or tiger cat (*Dasyurus maculatus*), reaches almost a metre in length, making it the longest carnivorous marsupial in the world. After the Tasmanian devil, it is the second largest marsupial carnivore alive today, with males weighing up to 3.5 kilograms. They have brown fur with white spots and a bright pink nose. The tiger quoll is native to the forests of eastern Australia and Tasmania, and has a life expectancy of just five years. They feed on possums, bandicoots, birds and small wallabies, hunting these tree-dwelling animals at night. They have ridged paws which make them well-suited for climbing trees.

Tiger quolls mate during winter, and sex can last for up to twenty-four hours! During this time, the male will grip the female's neck with his teeth, which can cause swelling and bleeding. In extreme cases, the female can die from wounds sustained during intercourse. There are five other species of quoll, living in either Australia or New Guinea. Sadly, these animals are under threat from habitat loss, as well as competition with foxes and cats, which have been introduced to their habitat. In Victoria, the quoll population has decreased by as much as half.

Axolotl:

The axolotl (*Ambystoma mexicanum*) is a critically endangered salamander that is only found in the lake complex of Xochimilco near Mexico City. Unlike most salamanders, they spend their whole lives in the water, and retain their larval form in adulthood. They are normally grey, or brown in colour, and have external gills on their heads. They feed on insects, molluscs and fish, and can change their colour slightly to blend in more with their surroundings. The average body length is about twenty centimetres, although axolotls measuring half a metre have been recorded.

The axolotl has the extraordinary ability to regenerate lost body parts, such as their limbs and tail. Even their spine can be regrown, and the regenerated structures are a perfect replicate of the original, with no scarring present. It is thought that they can regrow a limb over one hundred times! These salamanders are on the brink of extinction due to a combination of habitat loss, pollution, hunting and competition with invasive species. They were once present in Lake Chalco, but this body of water has been drained by humans to prevent flooding, which completely destroyed the salamander population there. The government in Mexico City has tried to save the species by constructing 'axolotl shelters' and placing more protection on their habitat, although this might be too late. Now, axolotls are extremely hard to find, and they might already be extinct in the wild.

Guianan Cock-of-the-Rock:

   This odd-looking bird is the Guianan cock-of-the-rock (*Rupicola rupicola*), which is native to the mountain forests of northern South America. Its main food source is fruit, but it also consumes small frogs, lizards and insects. Adults reach thirty centimetres in length. Males have spectacular bright orange plumage and large crests on their heads, which they develop after the age of three. Like most birds, the females are not as brightly coloured as the males, and are almost brown in colour (they also have a smaller crest).

   During the breeding season, males gather in groups of up to forty individuals, and take part in elaborate courtship displays, almost like a 'dance-off'. Females watch these performances and choose their mate by pecking at the male's back. The males' orange feathers and crest help to attract the opposite sex. This bird's bright colouration also stands out to predators such as eagles, boa constrictors and jaguars, so the male is more vulnerable to predation. The cock-of-the-rock makes cup-shaped nests and positions them on rocky cliffs, using its saliva to glue them into place. Although it has an extensive population, research suggests its numbers are slowly falling.

Giant Water Bug:

Giant water bugs (*Belostomatidae*) are one of the largest insects in the world, growing to over twelve centimetres in length. They can be found in ponds and streams in the Americas, East Asia and northern Australia. Due to their substantial size, they are able to take down large animals such as frogs, fish, baby turtles and even water snakes! They lurk at the bottom of a riverbed, and strike out whenever potential prey swim past. When it catches its victim, it will inject poisonous saliva from its piercing proboscis, digesting the animal from the inside. The giant water bug will normally wait for about fifteen minutes before eating, to allow the digestive enzymes to do their work. When the prey's insides have turned to mush, it will drink the fluids. Sometimes the bug will hunt in packs, and share their prey.

Giant water bugs store air under their wings and use these reserves to breathe whilst submerged, using tubes that protrude from their abdomen to extract air. Eggs are laid on the male's back, and he will guard them until they hatch, keeping them clean and moist. These bugs are also known as 'toe biters', and they have an excruciatingly painful bite. As a defence against large predators, they will secrete a liquid from their anus, and 'play dead', only to spring back to life and deliver a potent sting.

Cantor's Giant Softshell Turtle:

The endangered Cantor's giant softshell turtle (*Pelochelys cantorii*) is native to Southeast Asia, and has a face that resembles a frog. It is the largest freshwater turtle in the world, reportedly measuring up to two metres long, and weighing fifty kilograms. It lacks an external carapace and instead, has a 'soft' shell composed of thick skin covering broad, elongated ribs.

The giant softshell turtle has a rather unusual lifestyle, where it buries itself underground and lies motionless, with only its mouth poking out of the earth. It spends around ninety-five percent of its life like this, only emerging two times a day in order to breathe. This behaviour is useful as it keeps them hidden from prey, allowing them to burst out to catch nearby fish and crustaceans. The giant softshell has one of the quickest strikes in the animal kingdom, and is even faster than a king cobra! It has an incredibly strong bite that is capable of crunching through bone. Habitat loss, over-collection and hunting are just some of the factors that have resulted in this species becoming endangered. They are taken from the wild for the pet trade, and are hunted for their meat, eggs, and for use in traditional 'medicine'.

Water Bear:

One of the most versatile and extraordinary organisms on Earth is a microscopic, insect-like animal known as the water bear, or tardigrade (*Tardigrada*). They can be found in basically every environment on Earth. They are present on the tips of mountains, in volcanoes, in the deepest parts of the ocean, and in Antarctica. They have fat bodies with eight clawed legs, and grow to a mere half a millimetre in length. They are normally found on lichens and mosses, and eat tiny invertebrates, algae and other water bears.

There are over a thousand species of tardigrade, and they can withstand the most extreme environmental conditions. They are able to survive at temperatures as low as -272°C and as high as 150°C. They can withstand pressures six times as strong as those in the deepest oceans and can carry on as normal, after being exposed to vast amounts of ionizing radiation. They have been recorded living for ten days in space, even laying eggs there! The eggs hatched whilst in space and the baby water bears were healthy. These amazing creatures can even dry out to just three percent water and then spring back to life when rehydrated. If there's one species in this book that you don't need to worry about going extinct, it's the water bear!

Atolla Jellyfish:

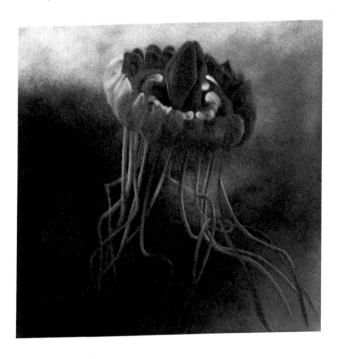

The Atolla jellyfish (*Atolla wyvillei*) lives in the deep sea between five hundred and five thousand metres from the surface. There are six species of *Atolla*, and they can be found in all of the world's oceans. Their red colour helps keep them hidden, as most organisms at those depths cannot see red light.

They grow to fifteen centimetres in diameter and have twenty tentacles. One of these tentacles is much larger than the others, and scientists think it might be used to catch food that floats by and to search for mates.

Atolla wyvillei has an unusual defence mechanism where it suddenly flashes with bioluminescence, changing colour to electric blue. This rapid colour change normally scares off the jellyfish's predators, but if it fails to do so, the light will often attract the attention of larger predators that will try and eat the original attacker. The commotion caused by these flashes allows the jellyfish to make a quick escape. Biologists have created a device that imitates the Atolla's flashing defence, and use it to lure elusive deep-sea predators (such as the giant squid – *Architeuthis*) so they can be filmed and studied.

Aye-Aye:

One of the world's strangest primates is the aye-aye (*Daubentonia madagascariensis*), endemic to the island of Madagascar. It is a type of lemur, and grows to about forty centimetres in length. It spends its entire life in the safety of the trees, and hunts at night for insects and fruit. In the daytime, aye-ayes sleep in an egg-shaped nest made of twigs and leaves. When foraging, they will tap on branches and tree trunks with their modified middle finger. This digit is very thin and flexible, and can be tapped up to eight times per second. Aye-ayes listen to the echoes created by their finger, to detect cavities in the tree where insects may be hiding. After finding a cavity, they will bite a hole in the wood and use their fourth finger (which is much longer than the others) to skewer and extract any burrowing insects inside, such as grubs. This hunting behaviour is known as 'percussive foraging' and is extremely rare in animals. Their elongated finger is also useful for removing flesh out of coconuts, and for piercing fruit.

Aye-ayes have strong opposable toes that allow them to cling onto branches. Their teeth are similar to a rodent's, and keep growing their whole lives. They are an endangered species, threatened by deforestation and hunting. In addition, farmers kill them because of the false belief that they damage crops, and others hunt aye-ayes because they perceive it as a bad omen.

Thorny Devil:

Thorny devils (*Moloch horridus*) are native to Australia and can grow to lengths of twenty centimetres. They feed exclusively on ants and will wait next to their trails, picking off the insects as quickly as one ant per second. The lizard's body is covered with dozens of thick spikes, which deter predators. They are camouflaged to their desert surroundings, and are able to change colour to better suit the environment. Heat also affects the colour of the lizard, and in the morning, they are covered in different shades of brown, which change to yellow as the temperature increases.

Thorny devils have an intriguing defence strategy, where they puff up their bodies to make themselves appear larger, and to make it harder for predators to pick them up. They also have a 'false head' to confuse predators. When attacked, they will lower their heads and expose a knobbly, head-like structure, keeping their actual skull safe. The lizard's spikes also collect water, and grooves between the spikes guide water droplets into its mouth. It is a slow walker, and will stop occasionally to wobble its body around, imitating desert vegetation blowing in the wind.

Hammerhead Worm:

Hammerhead worms (*Bipalium*) are bizarre creatures that are native to Oceania, Asia and Europe. They have also been introduced to the Americas, where they are considered an invasive species. They are land-based flatworms, and some species can grow to over a metre long! They have no circulatory or respiratory systems and also lack a skeleton. Their diet is made up entirely of earthworms, and they track their prey using chemoreceptors located on the underside of their heads. Hammerhead worms are vicious predators and latch onto worms, trapping them with their powerful muscles and a gluey substance that is excreted from the body. They can also inject a potent toxin to subdue their prey and to defend themselves against predators. After pinning down their prey, the hammerhead worm opens its mouth (which is actually located in the middle of its body) and expels a feeding cavity called the pharynx. The pharynx releases a set of enzymes to digest the earthworm from the outside, turning it into a liquid which it sucks into its body. Its mouth also serves as an anus, as this is where its waste is expelled.

The hammerhead worm can reproduce sexually, or asexually by removing its tail, which grows a head within ten days. After just two weeks, the severed tail will have transformed into a fully-grown adult. These flatworms are not endangered, and are actually threatening other species in areas where they have been introduced. They are an invasive species in France, and may impact soil ecology and plant health by reducing local populations of earthworms.

Horseshoe Crab:

Horseshoe crabs (*Limulidae*) are one of the most ancient animals, arising more than 450 million years ago. Four species exist today, which look like crustaceans, but are more closely related to spiders. They have ten eyes located all over their body, and their mouth is positioned on the underside, between the legs. A long, pointed tail is used to flip themselves over when they are stuck on their backs, as well as helping to steer when swimming.

Horseshoe crabs feed on algae, aquatic worms and the remains of dead animals. They live in shallow, muddy coastal waters, surfacing once a year to breed on the beach. Females lay eggs in the sand and males fertilise them as they are being laid. A single horseshoe crab can lay up to ninety thousand eggs in one sitting; however, only ten will survive to adulthood. These eggs are an important food source for birds, turtles and fish. The blood of horseshoe crabs contains special coagulates that humans use to check if medical equipment is sterile. The blood is harvested, and then they are released back into the wild. Sadly, some die during this process, and it is very stressful for the animals. Horseshoe crabs are declining in numbers due to hunting and coastal development.

Sea Bunny:

The sea bunny (*Jorunna parva*) is a type of nudibranch that can be found throughout the Indian and Pacific oceans, and grows to just two centimetres. There are thousands of species of nudibranch (also called sea slugs), which exhibit a huge variety of forms and colours. The sea bunny is so-called because of its white, fluffy appearance and presence of large 'ears' on the head. These 'ears' are actually rhinophores: organs that sense chemicals in the water. These structures allow the sea bunny to locate mates and food nearby, as well as sensing and responding to water currents. The 'tail' on the other side of the body is actually the slug's gills. A collection of small structures on the body called rods give the appearance of fur. The purpose of the rods is unknown, but they might also function as chemical detectors.

Like all species of nudibranch, sea bunnies are hermaphrodites, meaning they possess both male and female genitalia. When they mate, they exchange sperm and fertilise each other! They also have a spike that they jab into their partner during sex, to stop each other drifting away whilst mating. Their main food source is sponges, which contain high quantities of toxin. The nudibranch stores these toxins in its own body, making them poisonous to predators.

Mirror Spider:

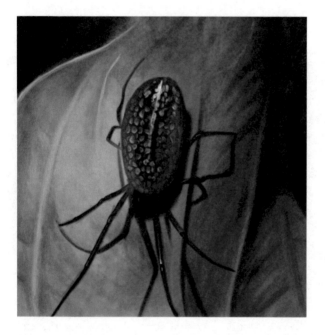

Mirror spiders, or sequined spiders (*Thwaitesia argentiopunctata*), are tropical arachnids native to the rainforests of Australia. They measure three millimetres in length, and their abdomens are adorned with reflective silver scales that look like little pieces of mirror. These scales are made of a reflective compound called guanine, and the spider can alter their size depending on its mood. When threatened, these metallic patches shrink and the colour of the abdomen beneath can be seen. At the end of the mirror spider's abdomen are a pair of fake eyes, which scares off potential predators. When the spider is relaxed and still, the reflective scales expand, filling up the abdomen. They also change size when the spider is on the move. There are at least twenty-two species of mirror spider, and some have gold or yellow mirror-like patches. Other species of arachnids that aren't closely related to the mirror spider also display these reflective abdomens. It is thought that these patches make the spider harder to spot by predators, as they scatter light.

Leaf Chameleon:

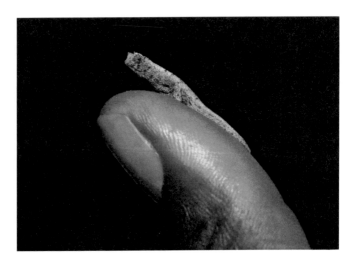

Discovered in 2012, the leaf chameleon (*Brookesia micra*) is the smallest known species of chameleon, and one of the smallest vertebrates on the planet. They live in the leaf litter and trees on a small island called Nosy Hara in Madagascar. Fully-grown adults have a maximum length of just 2.9 centimetres, which includes the tail. Scientists theorise that this may be the minimum size for an organism with complex eyes. They are so tiny, that they can fit on the head of a matchstick!

Leaf chameleons are active during the day and spend their time foraging on the forest floor, their brown bodies camouflaging them against the leaf-covered ground. When they are stressed, dark brown blotches appear all over their bodies. At night, they sleep in trees, five to ten centimetres off the ground. Unlike other chameleons, *Brookesia micra* uses its tail to support itself when climbing. Three other tiny species of chameleon reside on nearby islands, and they are thought to have shrunk due to a process called 'insular dwarfism'. This is where animals develop smaller bodies compared to their mainland relatives, in response to reduced food sources and habitat range. Reduced body size also allows for faster reproduction, which is an advantage on these small islands. *Brookesia micra* is a threatened species, and is susceptible to illegal logging and other disturbances. As their range is so tiny, it is crucial that their habitats are protected.

Red-Lipped Batfish:

The red-lipped batfish (*Ogcocephalus darwini*) is a strange fish native to the Galapagos Islands and the Peruvian coast. It grows to twenty centimetres long, and has bright red lips that look like they are covered in lipstick. The batfish's red lips might be used to entice mates and for recognising members of their own species. They have a long, pointed snout which is covered in hairs, and is used as a lure to attract prey, by releasing chemicals into the water. Its dorsal fin also functions as a lure, and develops into a long, thin appendage in adults. At the end of this structure is a light, which draws in animals nearby. This is an example of 'aggressive mimicry', where a predator imitates a harmless creature to deceive its prey and remain undetected. They feed on small fish, crabs and shrimp and wait for their prey to come to them.

Red-lipped batfish live on the sandy seafloor between three and seventy metres deep. They are bad swimmers, so instead, they use modified pelvic and pectoral fins to slowly 'walk' across the seafloor. The species is not currently threatened, as they live in a healthy environment that is relatively untouched by human development.

Bald-Headed Uakari:

Bald-headed uakaris (*Cacajao calvus*) are unusual primates found in a relatively small part of the Amazon rainforest in Peru and Brazil. They have a body length of forty-five centimetres, with a short, stumpy tail and shaggy, orange fur. The most striking feature of this monkey is its crimson-red, hairless head, which gains its colour from capillaries under the skin. A red face is a sign of good health, and is more attractive to mates. Those with pale faces are more likely to catch malaria, as they lack the genes that are responsible for resistance.

Bald-headed uakaris live in huge groups of up to one hundred individuals, and have a varied diet of fruit, seeds, flowers, leaves and insects. They spend most of their lives in the canopy and only come down to forage for nuts and seeds during the dry season. These monkeys are classed as vulnerable to extinction, and are one of the rarest primates in the Amazon. Their biggest threats are habitat loss and hunting. Much of the Amazon rainforest is being cut down, and human development is encroaching on the monkey's home.

Okapi:

The okapi (*Okapia johnstoni*) looks like a cross between a horse and a zebra, but it is actually more closely related to the giraffe. These animals inhabit dense forests in central Africa, in the northern regions of the Democratic Republic of the Congo. They stand at 1.5 metres tall and measure 2.5 metres in length. Their bodies are mainly brown in colour, but their legs are covered in white stripes which allows them to blend in amongst the thick vegetation. Males have horns measuring fifteen centimetres that are covered in hair. They are vegetarians, feeding on leaves, fungi, fruit and grass. Some of the plants they eat are poisonous, so in order to prevent toxins building up in the body, they consume charcoal, which acts as a natural antidote.

Okapis engage in a strange behaviour where they cross their legs in front of them and urinate all over themselves. They do this to pass their scent onto plants when they are walking through the forest, marking their territory. After birth, okapi babies will spend about two days following their mother, before building a nest. They will hide there for the next few months, sleeping and suckling, and growing rapidly. This species is endangered, and it faces many threats such as deforestation, illegal mining and poaching. The Okapi Conservation Project was set up in 1987 to combat the species' decline in numbers, and breeding programmes exist in a number of zoos.

References

AACC. "*Megalopyge opercularis.*" [online] Available at: https://www.aacc.org/community/divisions/tdm-and-toxicology/toxin-library/megalopyge-opercularis [Accessed 30 Nov. 2018].

Abrahamczyk, S, D Souto-Vilarós, and SS Renner. 2014. "Escape from extreme specialization: passionflowers, bats and the sword-billed hummingbird." *Proceedings of the Royal Society B: Biological Sciences* 281. 1795.

Akça, I, and C Tuncer. 2004. "Biological control and morphological studies on nut weevil (*Curculio nucum* L. Col., Curculionidae)." VI International Congress on Hazelnut 686.

Andrew, Deborah L. 2005. "Ecology of the tiger quoll *Dasyurus maculatus maculatus* in coastal New South Wales." *University of Wollongong.*

Arachne.org.au. "*Thwaitesia nigronodosa* (Rainbow, 1912) Black-spotted Thwaitesia (and *Thwaitesia argentiopunctata).*" [online] Available at: http://www.arachne.org.au/01_cms/details.asp?ID=2391 [Accessed 30 Nov. 2018].

Arkive. "Christmas frigatebird." [online] Available at: https://www.arkive.org/christmas-frigatebird/fregata-andrewsi/ [Accessed 30 Nov. 2018].

Arnold, Rachel J, Rob Harcourt and Theodore W Pietsch. 2014. "A new genus and species of the frogfish family Antennariidae (Teleostei: Lophiiformes: Antennarioidei) from New South Wales, Australia, with a diagnosis and key to the genera of the Histiophryninae." *Copeia* 2014 (3): 534-539.

Australian Government – Department of the Environment and Energy. "*Elusor macrurus* – Mary River turtle, Mary River tortoise." [online] Available at: http://www.environment.gov.au/cgi-bin/sprat/public/publicspecies.pl?taxon_id=64389 [Accessed 30 Nov. 2018].

Bay, Nicky. 2013. "Transformation of the mirror spider." [online] nickybay.com. Available at: https://www.nickybay.com/2013/07/transformation-of-mirror-spider.html [Accessed 30 Nov. 2018].

BBC Two. "Bizarre giraffe-necked weevils fight for a mate – Madagascar, preview – BBC Two." [Retrieved 30 Nov. 2018].

Bellamy, Lawrence, Nadine Chapman, Kevin Fowler, and Andrew Pomiankowski. 2013. "Sexual traits are sensitive to genetic stress and predict extinction risk in the stalk-eyed fly, *Diasemopsis meigenii*." *Evolution* 67 (9): 2662-2673.

Best, Robin C, and Ana Y Harada. 1985. "Food habits of the silky anteater (*Cyclopes didactylus*) in the central Amazon." *Journal of Mammalogy,* 66 (4): 780-781.

Binetti, Valerie R, Jessica D Schiffman, Oren D Leaffer, Jonathan E Spanier, and Caroline L Schauer. 2009. "The natural transparency and piezoelectric response of the *Greta oto* butterfly wing." *Integrative Biology* 1 (4): 324-329.

Boettcher, KJ, EG Ruby, and MJ McFall-Ngai. 1996. "Bioluminescence in the symbiotic squid *Euprymna scolopes* is controlled by a daily biological rhythm." *Journal of Comparative Physiology A* 179 (1): 65-73.

Bowen, WD, OT Oftedal, and DJ Boness. 1985. "Birth to weaning in 4 days: remarkable growth in the hooded seal, *Cystophora cristata*." *Canadian Journal of Zoology* 63 (12):2841-2846.

Brooke, Anne P. 1990. "Tent selection, roosting ecology and social organization of the tent-making bat, *Ectophylla alba*, in Costa Rica." *Journal of Zoology* 221 (1): 11-19.

Brusca, Richard C, and Matthew R Gilligan. 1983. "Tongue replacement in a marine fish (*Lutjanus guttatus*) by a parasitic isopod (Crustacea: Isopoda)." *Copeia* 1983 (3): 813-816.

Butler, Rhett A. 2012. "'Penis snake' discovered in Brazil is actually a rare species of amphibian." [online] Mongabay. Available at: https://news.mongabay.com/2012/08/penis-snake-discovered-in-brazil-is-actually-a-rare-species-of-amphibian/ [Accessed 2 Dec. 2018].

Carroll, Robert L. 1991. "10 The Origin of Reptiles." *Origins of the higher groups of tetrapods: controversy and consensus*: 331.

Catania, Kenneth C. 2005. "Star-nosed moles." *Current Biology* 15 (21): R863-R864.

Contreras, Victoria, Enrique Martínez-Meyer, Elsa Valiente, and Luis Zambrano. 2009. "Recent decline and potential distribution in the last remnant area of the microendemic Mexican axolotl (*Ambystoma mexicanum*)." *Biological conservation* 142 (12):2881-2885.

Corbett, LK. 1975. "Geographical distribution and habitat of the marsupial mole, *Notoryctes typhlops*." *Journal of the Australian Mammal Society* 1975; 1(4): 375-8.

Creighton, Jolene. (2016). "Making a monster: black dragonfish, the alien of the deep." [online] Futurism. Available at: https://futurism.com/aliens-of-the-deep-the-black-dragonfish [Accessed 8 Dec. 2018].

Cronin, Thomas W, and N Justin Marshall. 1989. "A retina with at least ten spectral types of photoreceptors in a mantis shrimp." *Nature* 339 (6220): 137.

Delsuc, Frédéric, Mariella Superina, Marie-Ka Tilak, Emmanuel JP Douzery, and Alexandre Hassanin. 2012. "Molecular phylogenetics unveils the ancient evolutionary origins of the enigmatic fairy armadillos." *Molecular Phylogenetics and Evolution* 62 (2): 673-680.

Dentressangle, Fabrice, Lourdes Boeck, and Roxana Torres. 2008. "Maternal investment in eggs is affected by male feet colour and breeding conditions in the blue-footed booby, *Sula nebouxii*." *Behavioral Ecology and Sociobiology* 62 (12): 1899-1908.

Dindal, Daniel L. 1970. "Feeding behavior of a terrestrial turbellarian *Bipalium adventitium*." *American Midland Naturalist*: 635-637.

Drummond, Hugh, and Cecilia Garcia Chavelas. 1989. "Food shortage influences sibling aggression in the blue-footed booby." *Animal Behaviour* 37: 806-819.

Duplaix, Nicole. (2007). "IUCN OSG – *Pteronura brasiliensis*." [online] IUCN Otter Specialist Group. Available at: http://www.otterspecialistgroup.org/Species/Pteronura_brasiliensis.html [Accessed 30 Nov. 2018].

EDGE of Existence. "Mary River turtle | *Elusor macrurus*." [online] Available at: http://www.edgeofexistence.org/species/mary-river-turtle/ [Accessed 6 Dec. 2018].

EDGE of Existence. "Purple frog | *Nasikabatrachus sahyadrensis*." [online] Available at: http://www.edgeofexistence.org/species/purple-frog/ [Accessed 30 Nov. 2018].

Engelhaupt, Erika. (2016). "Bizarre-looking beetle has an even weirder sex life." [online] National Geographic. Available at: https://news.nationalgeographic.com/2016/10/rare-weird-insect-trilobite-beetle/ [Accessed 30 Nov. 2018].

Erickson, Carl J. 1991. "Percussive foraging in the aye-aye, *Daubentonia madagascariensis*." *Animal Behaviour* 41 (5): 793-801.

Erwin, Douglas H, Marc Laflamme, Sarah M Tweedt, Erik A Sperling, Davide Pisani, and Kevin J Peterson. 2011. "The Cambrian conundrum: early divergence and later ecological success in the early history of animals." *science* 334 (6059): 1091-1097.

Fish Laboratory. "Fangtooth moray eel." [online] Available at: http://fishlaboratory.com/fish/fangtooth-moray-eel [Accessed 30 Nov. 2018].

Florida Fish and Wildlife Conservation Commission. "Facts about horseshoe crabs." [online] Available at: http://myfwc.com/research/saltwater/crustaceans/horses hoe-crabs/facts/ [Accessed 30 Nov. 2018].

Frogfish.ch. "*Antennarius multiocellatus*." [online] Available at: https://www.frogfish.ch/species-arten/Antennarius-multiocellatus.html [Accessed 30 Nov. 2018].

Gagyi-Palffy, Andrea, and Laurenţiu C Stoian. 2011. "A short review on tardigrades – some lesser known taxa of polyextremophilic invertebrates." *Extreme Life, Biospeology and Astrobiology* 3 (1): 13-26.

Galliez, Maron, Melina de Souza Leite, Thiago Lopes Queiroz, and Fernando Antonio dos Santos Fernandez. 2009. "Ecology of the water opossum *Chironectes minimus* in Atlantic forest streams of southeastern Brazil." *Journal of Mammalogy* 90 (1): 93-103.

Gibbons, John RH. 1981. "The biogeography of Brachylophus (Iguanidae) including the description of a new species, *B. vitiensis*, from Fiji." *Journal of Herpetology*: 255-273.

Girard, Madeline B, Michael M Kasumovic, and Damian O Elias. 2011. "Multi-modal courtship in the peacock spider, *Maratus volans* (OP-Cambridge, 1874)." *PLoS One* 6 (9): e25390.

Girons, H Saint, Ben D Beli, and Donald G Newman. 1980. "Observations on the activity and thermoregulation of the tuatara, *Sphenodon punctatus* (Reptilia: Rhynchocephalia), on Stephens Island." *New Zealand journal of zoology* 7 (4): 551-556.

Gordon, Malcolm S, Jeffrey B Graham, and Tobias Wang. 2004. "Introduction to the special collection: Revisiting the vertebrate invasion of the land." *Physiological and Biochemical Zoology* 77 (5): 697-699.

Groves, Paul. 1998. "Leafy sea dragons." *Scientific American* 279 (6):84-89.

Happold, DCD. 1967. "Biology of the jerboa, *Jaculus jaculus butleri* (Rodentia, Dipodidae), in the Sudan." *Journal of Zoology* 151 (2): 257-275.

Hart, JA, and TB Hart. 1990. "A summary report on the behaviour, ecology and conservation of the okapi (*Okapia johnstoni*) in Zaire." *Nature et Faune (FAO/PNUE) fre (Jul-Sep 1990) v. 6 (3) p. 21-28, 48-52.*

Heinrich, Sarah, Talia A Wittmann, Thomas AA Prowse, Joshua V Ross, Steven Delean, Chris R Shepherd, and Phillip Cassey. 2016. "Where did all the pangolins go? International CITES trade in pangolin species." *Global Ecology and Conservation* 8: 241-253.

Herring, PJ. 1990. "Bioluminescent responses of the deep-sea scyphozoan *Atolla wyvillei*." *Marine Biology* 106 (3): 413-417.

Hervant, Frédéric, Jacques Mathieu, and Jacques Durand. 2001. "Behavioural, physiological and metabolic responses to long-term starvation and refeeding in a blind cave-dwelling (*Proteus anguinus*) and a surface-dwelling (*Euproctus asper*) salamander." *Journal of Experimental Biology* 204 (2): 269-281.

Hoffner, Erik. (2018). "Only 12 vaquita porpoises remain, watchdog group reports." [online] Mongabay. Available at: https://news.mongabay.com/2018/03/only-12-vaquita-porpoises-remain-watchdog-groups-report/ [Accessed 30 Nov. 2018].

Hubbs, Carl L. 1958. "*Ogcocephalus darwini*, a new batfish endemic at the Galapagos Islands." *Copeia*: 161-170.

Igea, Javier, Pere Aymerich, Angel Fernández-González, Jorge González-Esteban, Asunción Gómez, Rocío Alonso, Joaquim Gosálbez, and Jose Castresana. 2013. "Phylogeography and postglacial expansion of the endangered semi-aquatic mammal *Galemys pyrenaicus*." *BMC evolutionary biology* 13 (1): 115.

IUCN Red List. "Marvelous spatuletail." [online] Available at: https://www.iucnredlist.org/species/22688130/93183168 [Accessed 30 Nov. 2018].

Ivlev, Yu F, MV Rutovskaya, and OS Luchkina. 2013. "The use of olfaction by the Russian desman (*Desmana moschata* L.) during underwater swimming." Doklady Biological Sciences.

Jolivet, Pierre. 1994. "Physiological colour changes in tortoise beetles." In *Novel aspects of the biology of Chrysomelidae* – 331-335. Springer.

Karplus, I, GC Fiedler, and P Ramcharan. 1998. "The intraspecific fighting behavior of the Hawaiian boxer crab, *Lybia edmondsoni*-fighting with dangerous weapons?" *Symbiosis-Rehovot* – 24: 287-302.

Kirkpatrick, RC, HJ Gu, and XP Zhou. 1999. "A preliminary report on Sichuan snub-nosed monkeys (*Rhinopithecus roxellana*) at Baihe Nature Reserve." *Folia Primatologica* 70 (2): 117-120.

Kock, Richard A, Mukhit Orynbayev, Sarah Robinson, Steffen Zuther, Navinder J Singh, Wendy Beauvais, Eric R Morgan, Aslan Kerimbayev, Sergei Khomenko, and Henny M Martineau. 2018. "Saigas on the brink: Multidisciplinary analysis of the factors influencing mass mortality events." *Science advances* 4 (1):eaao2314.

Kovacs, Kit M. 1990. "Mating strategies in male hooded seals (*Cystophora cristata*)?" *Canadian Journal of Zoology* 68 (12): 2499-2502.

Krugerpark.co.za. "Lilac breasted roller" [online] Available at: http://www.krugerpark.co.za/africa_lilac_breasted_roller.html [Accessed 8 Dec. 2018].

Lee, Jane J. (2015). "Meet the adorable 'sea bunny' taking over the internet." [online] National Geographic. Available at: https://news.nationalgeographic.com/2015/07/150723-

sea-slug-nudibranch-sea-bunny-ocean-animals-science/ [Accessed 8 Dec. 2018].

Lilia, K, Y Rosnina, H Abd Wahid, ZZ Zahari, and M Abraham. 2010. "Gross anatomy and ultrasonographic images of the reproductive system of the Malayan tapir (*Tapirus indicus*)." *Anatomia, histologia, embryologia* 39 (6): 569-575.

Lindberg, Annika Büchert, and Jens Mogens Olesen. 2001. "The fragility of extreme specialization: *Passiflora mixta* and its pollinating hummingbird *Ensifera ensifera*." *Journal of Tropical Ecology* 17 (2): 323-329.

Luo, Zhe-Xi, Alfred W Crompton, and Ai-Lin Sun. 2001. "A new mammaliaform from the early Jurassic and evolution of mammalian characteristics." *Science* 292 (5521): 1535-1540.

Mah, Christopher. (2009). "The sea pig *(Scotoplanes globosa)*." [online] Echinoblog. Available at: http://echinoblog.blogspot.com/2009/07/because-you-demanded-it-sea-pig-aka.html [Accessed 30 Nov. 2018].

Marshall, Christopher D, and John F Eisenberg. 1996. "*Hemicentetes semispinosus*." *Mammalian species* (541): 1-4.

Matsubayashi, Hisashi, Edwin Bosi, and Shiro Kohshima. 2003. "Activity and habitat use of lesser mouse-deer (*Tragulus javanicus*)." *Journal of Mammalogy* 84 (1): 234-242.

Mayor, P, J Mamani, D Montes, C González-Crespo, MA Sebastián, and M Bowler. 2015. "Proximate causes of the red face of the bald uakari monkey (*Cacajao calvus*)." *Royal Society open science* 2 (7).

McGovern, John P, Gilbert D Barkin, Thomas R McElhenney, and Reubin Wende. 1961. "*Megalopyge opercularis*: observations of its life history, natural history of its sting in man, and report of an epidemic." *JAMA* 175 (13): 1155-1158.

Middendorf III, George A, and Wade C Sherbrooke. 1992. "Canid elicitation of blood-squirting in a horned lizard (*Phrynosoma cornutum*)." *Copeia*: 519-527.

Miller, George C. 1967. "A new species of western Atlantic armored searobin, *Peristedion greyae* (Pisces: Peristedii dae.)" *Bulletin of Marine Science* 17 (1):16-41.

Milner-Gulland, EJ, and Navinder J Singh. 2016. "Two decades of saiga antelope research: What have we learnt?" *Antelope Conservation: From Diagnosis to Action* (16): 297.

Mori, Akira, and Tsutomu Hikida. 1994. "Field observations on the social behavior of the flying lizard, *Draco volans sumatranus*, in Borneo." *Copeia*: 124-130.

National Geographic. "Matschie's tree kangaroo." [online] Available at: https://www.nationalgeographic.com/animals/mammals/m/matschies-tree-kangaroo/. [Accessed 8 Dec. 2018].

Nielsen, Julius, Rasmus B Hedeholm, Jan Heinemeier, Peter G Bushnell, Jørgen S Christiansen, Jesper Olsen, Christopher Bronk Ramsey, Richard W Brill, Malene Simon, and Kirstine F Steffensen. 2016. "Eye lens radiocarbon reveals centuries of longevity in the Greenland shark (*Somniosus microcephalus*)." *Science* 353 (6300): 702-704.

Nogueira, José Carlos, Antonio Carlos S Castro, Edeltrudes Vieira C Câmara, and Bruno Garzon O Câmara. 2004. "Morphology of the male genital system of *Chironectes minimus* and comparison to other didelphid marsupials." *Journal of Mammalogy* 85 (5): 834-841.

Novarino, Wilson, and Rufford Small Grant. 2005. "Population monitoring and study of daily activities of Malayan tapir (*Tapirus indicus*)." *Report to Rufford Small Grant (for Nature Conservation) in Association with the Whitley Laing Foundation* 14: 28-30.

Oiseaux-birds.com. "Guianan cock-of-the-rock". [online] Available at: http://www.oiseaux-birds.com/cardguianan-cock-of-the-rock.html [Accessed 30 Nov. 2018].

Olson, Eric. 2015. "Featured creature: Hummingbird hawk-moth." [online] PBS Nature. Available at: http://www.pbs.org/wnet/nature/blog/featured-creature-hummingbird-hawk-moth/ [Accessed 30 Nov. 2018].

Patek, SN, WL Korff, and RL Caldwell. 2004. "Biomechanics: deadly strike mechanism of a mantis shrimp." *Nature* 428 (6985): 819.

Pianka, Eric R, and Helen D Pianka. 1970. "The ecology of *Moloch horridus* (Lacertilia: Agamidae) in western Australia." *Copeia*: 90-103.

Pierson, Elizabeth D, and William E Rainey. 1992. "The biology of flying foxes of the genus Pteropus: a review." Pacific island flying foxes: proceedings of an international conservation conference.

Rabb, George B, and Mary S Rabb. 1960. "On the mating and egg-laying behavior of the Surinam toad, *Pipa pipa*." *Copeia* 1960 (4): 271-276.

Robison, Bruce H, and Kim R Reisenbichler. 2008. "*Macropinna microstoma* and the paradox of its tubular eyes." *Copeia* 2008 (4): 780-784.

Robison, Bruce H, Kim R Reisenbichler, James C Hunt, and Steven HD Haddock. 2003. "Light production by the arm tips of the deep-sea cephalopod *Vampyroteuthis infernalis*." *The Biological Bulletin* 205 (2): 102-109.

Scudder, GGE. 1992. "The distribution and life cycle of *Reduvius personatus* (L.)(Hemiptera: Reduviidae) in Canada." *Journal of the Entomological Society of British Columbia* 89: 38-42.

Sergeant, DE. 1973. "Biology of white whales (*Delphinapterus leucas*) in western Hudson Bay." *Journal of the Fisheries Board of Canada* 30 (8): 1065-1090.

Smith, Robert L. 1997. "Evolution of paternal care in the giant water bugs (Heteroptera: Belostomatidae)." *The evolution of social behavior in insects and arachnids*: 116-149.

Smith, Tamara L, G David E Povel, and Kenneth V Kardong. 2002. "Predatory strike of the tentacled snake (*Erpeton tentaculatum*)." *Journal of Zoology* 256 (2): 233-242.

Snow, DW. 1971. "Notes on the biology of the cock-of-the-rock (*Rupicola rupicola*)." *Journal of Ornithology* 112 (3): 323-333.

Solis, M Alma, Shen-Horn Yen, John H Goolsby, Tony Wright, Robert Pemberton, Ampom Winotai, Usanee Chattrukul, Amara Thagong, and Suriont Rimbut. 2005. "*Siamusotima aranea*, a new stem-boring musotimine (Lepidoptera: Crambidae) from Thailand feeding on *Lygodium flexuosum* (Schizaeaceae)." *Annals of the Entomological Society of America* 98 (6): 887-895.

Steffen, Angie. "*Balaeniceps rex* (shoebill)." [online] Animal Diversity Web. Available at: https://animaldiversity.org/accounts/Balaeniceps_rex/ [Accessed 2 Dec. 2018].

Stevenson, Colin, and Romulus Whitaker. 2010. "Gharial *Gavialis gangeticus*." *Crocodiles. Status Survey and Conservation Action Plan*: 139-143.

Superina, Mariella. 2006. "New information on population declines in pink fairy armadillos." *Edentata*: 48-50.

Swart, CC, LE Deaton, and BE Felgenhauer. 2006. "The salivary gland and salivary enzymes of the giant waterbugs (Heteroptera; Belostomatidae)." *Comparative Biochemistry and Physiology Part A: Molecular & Integrative Physiology* 145 (1): 114-122.

Theuerkauf, Jörn, Sophie Rouys, Jean Marc Mériot, and Roman Gula. 2009. "Group territoriality as a form of cooperative breeding in the flightless Kagu (*Rhynochetos jubatus*) of New Caledonia." *The Auk* 126 (2): 371-375.

Tirtaningtyas, Fransisca N, and Janos C Hennicke. 2015. "Threats to the critically endangered Christmas Island frigatebird *Fregata andrewsi* in Jakarta Bay, Indonesia, and implications for reconsidering conservation priorities." *Marine Ornithology* 43: 137-140.

Towns, David R, G Richard Parrish, Claudine L Tyrrell, Graham T Ussher, Alison Cree, Donald G Newman, A H Whitaker, and Ian Westbrooke. 2007. "Responses of tuatara (*Sphenodon punctatus*) to removal of introduced Pacific rats from islands." *Conservation Biology* 21 (4): 1021-1031.

Uchida, Hiro'omi, Hidetomo Tanase, and Shin Kubota. 2009. "An extraordinarily large specimen of the polychaete worm *Eunice aphroditois* (Pallas) (Order Eunicea) from Shirahama, Wakayama, central Japan." *Kuroshio Biosphere* 5:9-15

Uiblein, F, JP Durand, C Juberthie, and J Parzefall. 1992. "Predation in caves: the effects of prey immobility and darkness on the foraging behaviour of two salamanders, *Euproctus asper* and *Proteus anguinus*." *Behavioural processes* 28 (1-2): 33-40.

van Dijk, Jiska. 2008. "Wolverine foraging strategies in a multiple-use landscape." *Norwegian University of Science and Technology*.

Vencl, Fredric V, Timothy C Morton, Ralph O Mumma, and Jack C Schultz. 1999. "Shield defense of a larval tortoise beetle." *Journal of chemical ecology* 25 (3): 549-566.

Verna, Caroline, Alban Ramette, Helena Wiklund, Thomas G Dahlgren, Adrian G Glover, Françoise Gaill, and Nicole Dubilier. 2010. "High symbiont diversity in the bone-eating worm *Osedax mucofloris* from shallow whale-falls in the North Atlantic." *Environmental microbiology* 12 (8): 2355-2370.

Villeneuve, Andrew. 2015. "Habitat selection, behavior, and natural history of the newly described leaf chameleon *Brookesia micra* (Reptilia, Squamata, Chamaeleontidae; Glaw, Köhler, Townsend

& Vences, 2012) on Nosy Hara, Madagascar." *Bowdoin College.*

Voss, S Randal, Hans H Epperlein, and Elly M Tanaka. 2009. "*Ambystoma mexicanum*, the axolotl: a versatile amphibian model for regeneration, development, and evolution studies." *Cold Spring Harbor Protocols* 2009 (8): pdb. emo128.

Walls, Elizabeth A, Jim Berkson, and Stephen A Smith. 2002. "The horseshoe crab, *Limulus polyphemus*: 200 million years of existence, 100 years of study." *Reviews in Fisheries Science* 10 (1): 39-73.

Wang, Xiao-ming, Ke-jia Zhang, Zheng-huan Wang, You-zhong Ding, Wei Wu, and Song Huang. 2004. "The decline of the Chinese giant salamander *Andrias davidianus* and implications for its conservation." *Oryx* 38 (2): 197-202.

Webb, Robert G. 2002. "Observations on the giant softshell turtle, *Pelochelys cantorii*, with description of a new species." *Hamadryad-Madras*- 27: 99-107.

Weishampel, David B, Peter Dodson, and Halszka Osmólska. 2007. *The dinosauria*: Univ of California Press.

Western Australian Museum. "Turtle frog | Western Australian museum." [online] Available at: http://museum.wa.gov.au/explore/frogwatch/frogs/turtle-frog [Accessed 2 Dec. 2018].

Wignall, Anne E, and Phillip W Taylor. 2009. "Alternative predatory tactics of an araneophagic assassin bug (*Stenolemus bituberus*)." *Acta ethologica* 12 (1): 23.

Wikelski, Martin, and Karin Nelson. 2004. "Conservation of Galápagos marine iguanas (*Amblyrhynchus cristatus*)." *Iguana* 11 (4): 190-197.

Wilkinson, Mark, and Ronald A Nussbaum. 1997. "Comparative morphology and evolution of the lungless caecilian *Atretochoana eiselti* (Taylor)(Amphibia: Gymnophiona: Typhlonectidae)." *Biological Journal of the Linnean Society* 62 (1): 39-109.

Wischusen, E William, and Milo E Richmond. 1998. "Foraging ecology of the Philippine flying lemur

(*Cynocephalus volans*).” *Journal of Mammalogy* 79 (4): 1288-1295.

WWF. 2018. *How many species are we losing?* [online] Available   at: http://wwf.panda.org/our_work/biodiversity/biodiversit y/ [Accessed 30 Nov. 2018].

Yano, K, JD Stevens, and LJV Compagno. 2007. “Distribution, reproduction and feeding of the Greenland shark *Somniosus* (Somniosus*) microcephalus*, with notes on two other sleeper sharks, *Somniosus* (Somniosus) *pacificus* and *Somniosu s* (Somniosus) *antarcticus*.” *Journal of fish biology* 70 (2): 374-390.

Yano, Kazunari, Masaki Miya, Masahiro Aizawa, and Tetsuhisa Noichi. 2007. “Some aspects of the biology of the goblin shark, *Mitsukurina owstoni*, collected from the Tokyo Submarine Canyon and adjacent waters, Japan.” *Ichthyological Research* 54 (4): 388-398.

Zintzen, Vincent, Clive D Roberts, Marti J Anderson, Andrew L Stewart, Carl D Struthers, and Euan S Harvey. 2011. “Hagfishpredatory behaviour and slime defence mechanism.” *Scientific Reports* 1: 131.